Praise From Industry Leaders

"Kristina Powers has produced another set of outstanding insights. If you're looking for practical, proven ways to improve your organization's performance, this is the book for you."

Michael Conlin
Former Chief Data Officer of the US Department of Defense, CEO and Founder, Conlin Group LLC

"As a U.S. Army veteran, I learned early in my career the importance of having a Second-in-Command who can share leadership responsibilities. Unfortunately, higher education leaders and institutions need to fully grasp the importance of creating a management or leadership team model that prepares and allows multiple people to share responsibility. In *Second-in-Command, First in Excellence*, Dr. Powers provides secrets to achieving a team approach to organizational success that every leader or organization should know and practice. 2iC should be required reading for presidents, chief executive officers, and their direct reports as part of their institutional sustainability strategy."

Dr. Thomas Stewart
Executive Vice President for Social Justice, Equity, Diversity, and Inclusion (S-JEDI) at National University

"I've clearly seen the power of what we call a "Visionary/ integrator Duo" at the helm of an entrepreneurial company— given the right structure of "rules & tools" to blend their natural friction into a powerful, positive force. I'm excited to see KP leveraging a form of this combination within much larger organizations that traditionally struggle with much more bureaucracy than our otherwise nimble entrepreneurs."

Mark C. Winters
Co-author, *Rocket Fuel*

"So much is written about leadership that it is rare to get a new perspective that is game changing. This book contains that new perspective. If you want to leverage untapped potential in your organization and successfully navigate uncertainty, take the time to read this book. It will give you an advantage others aren't even aware of."

Danette Fenton-Menzies
Director of Learning, Magical Learning Pty Ltd

"*Second-in-Command, First in Excellence* is a remarkable study in leadership for current leaders and a primer for those on the leadership track. Dr. Kristina Powers demonstrates her years as an effective higher education leader by eloquently expressing her expertise gleaned through trial and practice at the highest levels of leadership. I highly recommend this book and predict that those serious about honing their leadership skills will keep a copy close at hand."

John Crawford
Principal, Coleman Talley Strategies

"Kristina 'KP' Powers has written an important book at a time of increasing volatility and complexity in the world. *Second-in-Command, First in Excellence* details a practical and actionable framework for organizations to establish a chain of high performing 2iCs. This chain acts as a safety net, delivering multiple benefits organization-wide within a short space of time. It drives autonomy and faster decision-making. It de-risks the organization against external pressures, as executives and senior leaders can maintain focus on strategic priorities. And, it diversifies the experience and development pathways of key talent, promoting employee retention. It is required reading for those looking to introduce 2iCs in their organization, or budding-2iCs seeking to take on the next, fulfilling professional challenge."

Sophie Krantz

Global Strategist and Exponential Organizational Practitioner

"Although the reasons for this have been taking shape for decades, recent years have seen the U.S. experience a crippling labor shortage. This crisis is part of a seismic and historically unprecedented shift in labor demographic dynamics. As America, and the world, move forward in their intensifying competition for talent, several themes will continue to emerge; how do you keep your best people, how do you develop those people to be your next generation of leaders, and how do you limit disruptions when those people leave? In Kristina 'KP' Powers' new book, she delves deep into one of these ways, namely, spreading the leadership qualities and expectations to multiple people called Seconds-in-Command or 2iCs. Recent research shows that increasingly people want jobs that a company and society values and that they will trade salary for that perceived value. By instilling leadership traits and responsibilities, companies can address all concerns at once. It is important to listen to the messages KP is discussing. Our future will require new solutions that our past could live without."

Ron Hetrick

Sr. Labor Economist and lead author of *Demographic Drought, Lightcast*

Second-in-Command (2iC), First in Excellence

Why do some departments, divisions, and organizations soar while others struggle? Watching another team achieve the success you feel yours more rightfully deserves can be incredibly frustrating. However, they might have something you don't: Seconds-in-Command.

Given how many Seconds-in-Command exist in the workforce, it is stunning that there are so few books about them. Organizations can and often do have more than one 2iC; large ones may have hundreds. KP Powers focuses on essential skills that individuals in these positions already possess and can enhance to become an organization's key to achieving phenomenal success.

This book introduces the groundbreaking concept of linking multiple 2iCs to form a Second-in-Command chain. This game-changing technique increases the positive impact that 2iCs can have on organizational and leader success.

In today's world, leaders no longer have the luxury of hiring more people to keep up with a growing workload. The labor shortage and the need to cut costs because of looming economic issues make that impractical. It makes more sense to consider a new organizational framework that includes 2iCs, thus multiplying existing team members' contributions. This is especially critical in highly regulated fields such as higher education, finance, and health care, where the stakes and penalties are high and unforgiving.

Second-in-Command, First in Excellence invites readers to think differently about this critical role. Geared toward leaders who have or want a 2iC as well as 2iCs themselves, this book both demonstrates the value of the 2iC position and serves as a tool for professional development.

Kristina 'KP' Powers, PhD, is an international author, trainer, and mentor. As a data expert, KP helps leaders combine and leverage their greatest assets—people and data—for success. Learn more at KPPowers.com

Second-in-Command (2iC), First in Excellence

An Organization's Secret to Achieving Phenomenal Success

Kristina 'KP' Powers, PhD

Foreword by
Colonel Chad M. Pillai

Routledge
Taylor & Francis Group

A PRODUCTIVITY PRESS BOOK

First published 2024
by Routledge
605 Third Avenue, New York, NY 10158

and by Routledge
4 Park Square, Milton Park, Abingdon, Oxon, OX14 4RN

Routledge is an imprint of the Taylor & Francis Group, an informa business

ISBN: 978-1-032-46508-1 (hbk)
ISBN: 978-1-032-46507-4 (pbk)
ISBN: 978-1-003-38200-3 (ebk)

DOI: 10.4324/9781003382003

Typeset in Garamond
by SPi Technologies India Pvt Ltd (Straive)

To all the big sisters who have little sisters. Thank you for pushing us little sisters further than our dreams could take us.

And

To my own big sister, Teresa.

Contents

Figures

Preface

Why do some departments, divisions, and organizations soar while others struggle? Watching another team achieve the success you feel yours more rightfully deserves can be incredibly frustrating. However, they might have something you don't: Seconds-in-Command.

The plural of Second-in-Command (2iC) is intentional in the sentence above. Organizations can and often do have more than one 2iC; large ones may have hundreds. Given how many Seconds-in-Command exist in the workforce, it is stunning that there are so few books about them. Having served as a 2iC myself, I focus on essential skills that individuals in these positions already possess and can enhance to become an organization's key to achieving phenomenal success. This book introduces the groundbreaking concept of linking multiple 2iCs to form a Second-in-Command chain. This game-changing technique increases the positive impact that 2iCs can have on organizational and leader success.

In today's world, leaders no longer have the luxury of hiring more people to keep up with a growing workload. The labor shortage and the need to cut costs because of the looming economic issues make that impractical. It makes more sense to consider a new organizational framework that includes 2iCs, thus multiplying existing team members' contributions. This is especially critical in highly regulated fields such as higher education, finance, and health care, where the stakes and penalties are high and unforgiving.

Second-in-Command, First in Excellence invites readers to think differently about this critical and largely overlooked role. Geared toward leaders who have or want a 2iC as well as 2iCs themselves, this book both demonstrates the value of the 2iC position and serves as a tool for professional development.

Inspiration for the Book

I wrote this book for three reasons: (1) to share this amazing "secret" with fellow leaders who want to achieve phenomenal success, (2) to elevate the role of Seconds-in-Command, and (3) to help other 2iCs better understand how the different aspects of their position fit together and how to develop their 2iC skills to the fullest.

I've written the book I would have wanted to read when I began my career more than two decades ago. I would have appreciated learning in college or high school that there was a "thing" called Second-in-Command, or 2iC for short. Unbeknownst to me, I had classic 2iC characteristics. It was by writing this book that I finally came to understand how many disparate interests and skill sets converge in this role.

Over my 20-plus years of living in five states, working in seven cities, and consulting throughout the country and internationally, one question has continued to dog me: Why do some departments, divisions, and organizations soar while others struggle? As a researcher, I've studied this issue from every possible angle—reading, asking questions, observing, analyzing, forming hypotheses, reading more, asking more questions, observing more, and analyzing more. I've synthesized my resulting knowledge, informed by hands-on experience as a 2iC, into this book to advance the work of other ambitious leaders.

Foreword

History is replete with consequential political, military, and business leaders. However, few consider the role that Seconds-in-Command (2iCs) play in the success of their bosses and organizations. Most 2iCs remain in the background, while some rise to prominence. Harry S. Truman comes to mind; having served as the 2iC to Franklin D. Roosevelt, he became an equally significant president in his own right.

Connection With the Author

Dr. Kristina 'KP' Powers' book is a timely examination of the role of a 2iC. Dr. Powers and I have known each other since our first day of college more than 25 years ago. During our time together in college at SUNY Brockport, I briefly served as her 2iC as she spearheaded the establishment of the Delta College Student Association. Our paths after college diverged, hers to academia, data analytics, and organizational administration and mine to the military as an Army officer rising to the rank of colonel in 2022.

From 2iC to Colonel in the U.S. Army

Second-in-Command is a well-known and well-respected role in the military. Having served in the U.S. Army for 22 years, some of my most rewarding assignments have been as a 2iC.

My first 2iC assignment was as an executive officer stationed in South Korea. In that capacity, I was responsible to my commander for my company's operational readiness, ensuring that all the combat vehicles were maintained and the supply inventory accounted for while remaining prepared to assume command.

A key element to my success in South Korea was building strong relationships with my fellow 2iCs in my battalion, brigade, and division. The connections came in handy when I needed help obtaining the parts and tools required to maintain my company's high operational readiness rates. Relationship building is among the hallmark skill sets of a successful 2iC in the military. Rather than discussing relation-ship building as a stand-alone skill, KP incorporates it throughout her clever 2iC Excellence Framework.

In addition to relationship building, two additional skills I honed while serving as a 2iC in the military were planning and communication. It comes as no surprise that two of the four phases of KP's 2iC Excellence Framework are devoted to these important topics. If relationship building is the bedrock, then planning and communication are the founda-tion, especially in my current role as Chief of Plans for the U.S. Army.

I began to develop my expertise in planning and commu-nication during my second consequential 2iC assignment as the Deputy Director for Strategy, Plans, and Policy for a the-ater special operations command. In that position, I was responsible to my director for establishing the priority of the command's planning efforts; communicating with higher, adjacent, or subordinate headquarters; and ensuring transparency among adjacent staff directorates.

Additionally, I served as a quality control agent, providing quality products that were transmitted to the Director and the Commander. The concept of quality thus became a more dominant part of my thinking and strategy. It was my responsibility to ensure the quality. KP's 2iC Excellence Framework thoughtfully addresses quality in Phase D (Quality) with three stages (Trust but Verify, Crosschecking, and Protect Your #1).

Developing skills such that you are delivering high quality gets noticed—especially by your First-in-Command. As a result of my getting noticed, my final 2iC experience was as Deputy Director of a Commander's Action Group for a 4-Star Geographic Combatant Commander. As the 2iC, I ensured the group's priority of work, communicated the commander's requirements to subordinate commands and staff directorates, and briefly assumed the role of director supporting the commander during a crucial overseas mission to Iraq and Afghanistan.

That assignment taught me how a senior military leader interacted with U.S. and international political, diplomatic, and military leaders in a volatile world region. Supporting your First-in-Command during difficult and tense times is hard—there are no two ways about it. However, the emphasis on preparation, communication, and quality enables a 2iC to play a critical role in emergency situations. KP delves into this issue in the section on blazing new trails.

My experiences as a 2iC gave me the kind of essential lessons to support Firsts-in-Command as well as strengthen my leadership skills. These lessons align with a saying used in the Army: "Mission First, People Always!" KP addresses the importance of people—all people—in Phase C: Empathy.

Supporting Your First-in-Command—Words of Advice

A successful 2iC focuses on supporting the leader and the organization. As a 2iC, I sought to ensure that I understood and embraced my boss's vision and intent for accomplishing our assigned mission. Understanding and embracing my boss's vision and intent didn't always mean I agreed with every decision; it meant I provided my counsel when the opportunity presented itself and carried out the final decision when made. A leader gains the trust of their 2iC when the two can share and debate ideas and when the 2iC works to preserve flexibility and decision space for their boss. Such a relationship means that a 2iC shares their disagreements privately while showing support in public.

Anticipating Friction and Opportunities—Words of Advice

Another important trait for a successful 2iC is anticipating both friction and opportunities for the leader and the organization. As a 2iC, I strived to scan the horizon to mitigate potential friction points that could derail the successful completion of the mission. Examples from my career included anticipating shortfalls in maintenance parts that would have negatively impacted my company's operational readiness or identifying emerging bureaucratic requirements that required reprioritizing personnel work efforts.

Anticipating opportunities is equally important. I once recognized an officer's potential to successfully develop a new planning approach and raised the opportunity with my boss. Within months, the officer had successfully spearheaded a cross-functional planning effort that transformed the headquarters and its approach to the organization's mission.

A Duty of Care—Words of Advice

The third element of a successful 2iC is caring for the people in the organization. In some instances, the leader gets to play the good cop, while the 2iC plays the bad cop. However, in well-functioning organizations, both the leader and the 2iC have a role in ensuring the well-being and morale of their people. A successful 2iC balances the needs of the people in the organization with those of the leader. A successful partnership between a leader and a 2iC means that a 2iC focuses down and in, while the leader focuses up and out.

Throughout my career, I focused on the morale and development of the people in my organization. The approach I took was to inquire about the work people were performing, ask how I could help them succeed, and then endeavor to set the conditions for their future success. In my last 2iC job, I focused on identifying the aspirations of the people in my organization. Knowing that I cared about their future, the people in my organization remained high-spirited, which was reflected in the quality of their work.

2iC as a Perpetual Learner—Words of Advice

Finally, a successful 2iC is a leader in their own right and takes any opportunity to learn from someone else's experience and knowledge. Unlike in the Army, where someone will not serve as a 2iC in the unit they will command, my Navy brethren use a model where a 2iC serves on the ship or in the position over which they will assume command. The key lesson is that to be a successful leader, one must learn how to be led. Serving as a 2iC places you at the inflection point between the leader and the led.

Enhancing the Use of 2iCs in Your Organization

KP's book is essential in understanding the crucial role 2iCs play in all organizations—especially when a 2iC chain exists. The impact that multiple 2iCs connected together can have both on the First-in-Command and on the organization overall is significant. The lessons illustrated throughout the book are worth studying and restudying for those progressing through their career as well as for Firsts-in-Command that want to accelerate their successes. This book offers practical lessons on how successful organizations are managed and led through empowered and entrusted 2iCs.

—**Colonel Chad M. Pillai**, U.S. Army

Colonel Chad M. Pillai is a U.S. Army strategist who has completed multiple assignments in the U.S., Europe, the Middle East, and Northeast Asia. He served as a Visiting Defense Fellow at the Centre for International Defense Policy (CIDP) at Queen's University, Kingston, Canada and earned his master's degree from Johns Hopkins University School of Advanced International Studies (SAIS). The views expressed here are his and do not reflect the official position of the U.S. government and the Department of Defense.

Acknowledgments

I would like to express heartfelt appreciation to those who have made this book possible. First, it is with great gratitude that I thank my publisher: Taylor & Francis Group, especially Senior Editor Kristine Rynne Mednansky and her team. I am privileged to work on this sixth book with the dedicated and experienced teams at Taylor & Francis Group and Routledge Publishers.

I would like to thank the individuals who took the time to participate in an interview to develop the book. I have incorporated select quotes from some interviewees, which resulted in an enhanced and robust publication.

I deeply admire the editing expertise of Tracy Kendrick. Her attention to detail and passion for her profession was the patina that elevated the book. I was delighted when Tracy agreed to edit my book since her exceptional skills would bring out its strengths.

This book visually comes to life with much thanks to Diana Goldstein's design expertise for the figures throughout the book. Diana turned my hand-drawn images and rough draft artwork into polished and aesthetically pleasing figures that amplified critical messages throughout the book.

Last but not least, an honorable mention goes to my family and friends—especially my husband, Tim. With his support, I can complete the work I am so passionate about.

About the Author

KP Powers, PhD, is an international author, trainer, and mentor. As a data expert, KP helps leaders combine and leverage their greatest assets—people and data—for success.

Throughout her career and consulting engagements, KP has held positions that combined the duties of Second-in-Command and Chief Data Officer. In these roles, Dr. Powers brings together people, data, and information to help leaders deliver value to their customers, clients, and students through her strategic thinking and implementation expertise.

She uses her experience as a 2iC and her knowledge of data to help ambitious leaders build healthy data cultures, deliver value, and navigate disruption. KP's contributions on several boards have recognized her as a strategic thinker and leader. Learn more at KPPowers.com

Dr. Powers also is the President of the Institute for Effectiveness in Higher Education (IEHE)—an organization that elevates forward thinking to accelerate colleges and universities. In this role, she founded and launched the Accreditation Liaison Collaborative. Created by accreditation liaisons for accreditation liaisons, the Accreditation Liaison Collaborative provides a national resource to support Accreditation Liaisons throughout the country with professional development, access to materials that improve the quality of an institution's accreditation materials, and networks with other Accreditation Liaisons who have blazed trails. Learn more about IEHE at InstituteForEffectiveness.org

Originally from Buffalo, New York, KP has lived in five states (New York, North Carolina, Florida, Georgia, and California) and Washington, DC. She currently resides in San Diego, CA, with her husband, Tim, enjoying the warm weather, organic and gluten-free food, and as much travel as her schedule will allow.

You can connect with KP on LinkedIn, Twitter, Facebook, Instagram, or YouTube. If you would like to talk to KP about any advisory work, training, or mentoring, then you can contact her at KP@KPPowers.com

Why This Book?

Why do some departments, divisions, and organizations soar while others struggle? Watching another team achieve the success you feel yours more rightfully deserves can be incredibly frustrating. Even more maddening, you have read the best and latest leadership books and implemented "best practices."

Of the many leadership approaches described in books and utilized by executives, there are five that are common, thus, used regularly. Each standard leadership approach has its own pros, cons, and costs, to root out inefficiencies or ineffectiveness (Figure 1).

Choose Your Approaches Carefully

As a leader, you've likely used one or more—or all—of these leadership approaches yourself at some point. At the very least, you will have had some experience with them all during the course of your career. Each of these approaches can be effective when used properly. It's a question of using the right tool for the job. Using the wrong tool can make things worse, be a waste of time, or yield poor results, but the right tool makes it possible to accomplish hard work with pride and joy. Take do-it-yourself home improvement projects. I enjoy doing

DOI: 10.4324/9781003382003-1

Standard Leadership Approaches

	Pros	Cons
Shake–Up in Leadership/ Management — Reorganize leadership and/or terminate managers who are not getting the job done.	Introduces a fresh set of ideas and approaches with no politics to get in the way of progress.	It's costly and disruptive to change leadership and managers. This is usually the last resort due to the downtime resulting from removing the current leader, searching for a replacement, and giving the new person time to get up to speed. **$$$$**
Increase the Number of Employees — Add more people to the team to spread out the workload.	Spreading out the work allows leadership to spot any hiccups in the process.	It's costly to add permanent employees. Part-time or contract employees may not be as invested as their full-time counterparts. Time is lost in onboarding as well as in managing and communicating with a larger team. **$$$$**
Introduce New Technology — Streamline processes and reduce waste by adding new technology and software to solve problems.	If technology replaces repetitive tasks and/or can help reduce errors, then efficiency and effectiveness metrics are likely to improve.	If the issue is a people problem, rarely (and I mean rarely) is technology the solution. Adding new technology to the problem simply creates more problems. **$$$**
Invest in Training — Upskill employees so that they have the latest skill sets to do their jobs more efficiently and effectively.	Upskill employees so that they have the latest skill sets to do their jobs more efficiently and effectively.	Unclear which employees will want to learn new information and even fewer will actually use the information. Thus, the investment may not have as large of an impact as intended. **$$**
Step–Up Management — Get senior leaders and managers involved in the details to ensure employees remain focused on priorities and adhere to strict deadlines under a watchful eye.	The leader/manager at the next level-up sees the real problems and can either remove roadblocks or communicate needs upwards.	Being micromanaged for extended periods of time can be confusing for employees (e.g., who is the decision maker?). Micromanaging for extended periods of time can be very demotivating for employees, especially top performers. **$$**

KP Powers

Figure 1   Standard Leadership Approaches.

home renovations (both DIY and contracted out). I simply love the process of making something the best it can be—and then marveling at the results. I have many fond memories of working on house projects with my mom, the source of all of my DIY knowledge.

The Wrong Tools Make for a Miserable Experience

Once I was installing a bathroom faucet, a job I'd done plenty of times in different homes I'd owned. This time, though, I was doing it in a century-old home where we'd had all of the plumbing in the walls professionally replaced. I was looking forward to finishing our bathroom update and even had a flashback to the good times I'd had with my mom about a decade before, helping her change her kitchen faucet on a trip home to see her. My husband and I were "simply" install-ing a new vanity and hooking up the faucet and the drain. For any fellow-DIYers reading this, the drain was stubbed out and the water lines had angle stops. Since I was dealing with new plumbing, this "easy" faucet replacement was well within my wheelhouse. Plumbing is plumbing, right? Not quite.

A new installation is very different from a replacement. When you are replacing something, you have the previous parts to bring to the hardware store for sizes. Since I was flying blind, I spent way too much time in the plumbing aisle constructing a drain from the hundreds of pieces available. I finally finished the task after multiple trips to the hardware store but ended up disliking the whole project—a lot. Because I didn't have the right tools for the job, something that had once brought me joy and good memories had turned into an expensive ordeal in an aisle of the hardware store that I now avoid. I recently hired a plumber to replace the bath-room faucets in our new home.

There *Has* to Be Another Way

Even after utilizing the standard leadership approaches, and putting extensive hours in doing so, it can be extremely frustrating to still not make progress commensurate with the effort. At some point, a pause is needed to self-examine what is working as well as insist that there has to be another way.

The leadership approaches are great tools when they are the *right* tools. Some of the best books written on leadership fall into one of the five leadership approach categories. And many leaders and managers will attest that the leadership approaches deliver visible results. Having used all of the leadership approaches at some point in my own career, I agree.

Is that it, though? Are these the only five approaches available to leaders? At some point, recycling the five leadership approaches—and their sub-approaches—over and over again gets stale and unproductive. Arguably, some of the sub-approaches aren't even relevant anymore.

For example, cross-training employees was a common management approach. The idea was that companies had reduced risk if there were other employees who could fill in for each other in the event of an absence or departure. Additionally, employees would learn about each other's job such that there would be greater understanding and appreciation for others' work. It turned out that training employees to do jobs that they didn't care about, let alone weren't passionate about, was not very useful.

More importantly, ambitious leaders in a post-pandemic world have a new set of problems for which no playbook exists. Even if there were a playbook, things are changing so fast that it would soon be obsolete.

Yet somehow, some leaders are figuring it out—or at the very least appearing to. Maybe they have something you don't: a Second-in-Command.

What Is a Second-in-Command (2iC)?

If you haven't heard the term "Second-in-Command" (2iC) on the job before, you will surely have encountered such equivalents as "deputy" or "executive officer" (XO). Some may call the role a #2 (of course, that can have a different meaning, so I'll stick to 2iC). In its simplest sense, 2iC refers to the person in authority or command who is taking care of the details at the next layer down from the supervisor.

A Second-in-Command isn't just for CEOs anymore. If the C-suite wants excellence at every level of their organization, every leader, especially those that have employees reporting to them and/or budget authority, needs to have their own Second-in-Command.

> Ideally, what you want in a number two is somebody that can take over the job from you without any hiccups and, hopefully, do the job better than you can do it. If you're doing your job as the leader, you are developing other people, including your Second in Command

explains Robert Daugherty, The Holdings.

Why Have 2iCs in Your Organization?

With so many competing priorities, leaders have to weigh each decision carefully with value in mind, including whether to incorporate 2iCs into their organization. Figure 2 illustrates the value of 2iCs and 2iC chains (explained below) in six categories.

Going it Alone

Every organization, from a single department to a vast corporation, starts out with one person seeking to bring an idea or

Value of a 2iC Chain

Type and Description	# of People (including first in command)	Impact
2iC Chain Two or more trained 2iCs linked together and jointly committed to long-term success, delivering unparalleled results.	3+	10X+
Trained 2iC Complementary extension of you in all of the areas you prefer to hand off to a trained employee with tools and resources to advance your vision.	2	6X
Self-Taught 2iC You are committed for the long term, but learning on the job involves some trial and error and patience on your part.	2	3X

– – – – –Phenomenal Success Line– – – – –

Full-Time Employee Relief for you, but limited commitment from the employee. Some time needs to be reserved for non-project tasks.	2	1.75X
Part-Time Employee The person can reduce the workload on a particular set of tasks. However, time is still needed to train and prepare tasks.	1.5	1.25X
Going It Alone An exciting opportunity, an abyss of work and things to learn.	1	1X

KP Powers

Figure 2   Value of a 2iC Chain.

vision to fruition—this is the First-in-Command. Flying solo can be exciting at first, but the volume of work quickly becomes overwhelming. A single person simply doesn't have the ability and expertise to accomplish everything that needs to be done, all the while learning on the job. There is a limit to the impact that one person can have, hence the figures of 1X.

Part-Time Employee

The organization begins to grow such that revenues and operations require not only more person-time but also greater expertise (e.g., social media promotion, bookkeeping, administrative support). Since the organization is just starting to gain momentum, temporary/part-time support is approved because it is less costly than engaging a permanent full-time employee. While a part-time person may be hired, their impact combined with that of the First-in-Command might only be 1.25X rather than the expected 1.5X because the First-in-Command needs to slow down a bit to get the new employee up to speed.

Moreover, the part-time person is only selectively helpful because they cannot assist with all tasks. Their scope of work ends up being limited to the problems or areas that the First-in-Command needs the most help with. Often the First-in-Command will initially find it easier to keep doing things on their own, but it is important to devote the necessary time to training the new hire, taking one step back to take two steps forward.

Full-Time Employee

Many Firsts-in-Command feel like things will get significantly easier once operations can justify hiring a full-time employee since that person will be available to relieve the First-in-Command's workload as needed. However, the new hire's level of commitment to the department, organization, cause, and/or First-in-Command likely is limited. The employee does not have the same level of long-term commitment as the First-in-Command as they may see the position as only "a job." It is highly unlikely that the full-time hire will stay in the role for an extended period of time as the average time in professional (non-management) positions is around three to six years; some employees will stay less.

Additionally, the full-time employee and the First-in-Command will also have to deal with various regulatory matters to maintain compliance (e.g., sexual harassment training, timecards), reducing direct time spent on the organization's goals. As a result, the combined impact of a First-in-Command and full-time employee is only 1.75X, even though two people are involved.

Crossing Over the Line to Phenomenal Success

The overwhelming majority of organizations operate as solopreneurs (by design or temporarily) with part-time or full-time staff. Those that cross the Phenomenal Success line leverage Seconds-in-Command (2iCs), giving these employees greater agency and in turn the ability to have a greater stake in and greater impact on organizational outcomes. The three categories of 2iCs are described below.

Self-Taught 2iC

Some 2iCs naturally gravitate to the role without knowing its formal name. Self-taught 2iCs learn the skills and responsibilities of a 2iC on the job. Because the self-taught 2iC is intrinsically motivated to forge their own path to the position, they are typically committed for the long term. However, because they are learning on the job, trial and error occurs more frequently than necessary. Even so, combining a First-in-Command with a 2iC creates a multiplier impact of 3X with just two people.

Trained 2iC

As with any position, 2iC training adds value since the employee steps into the role with a base knowledge that the organization can leverage and build on, rather than starting from scratch. A trained 2iC receives targeted professional development to hone skills that correspond to the First-in-Command's needs and abilities. Trained 2iCs have the benefit of learning from 2iCs that came before them and obtaining a set of tools and resources to draw on in their dynamic role—without wasting time on trial and error. As with many professions, a trained 2iC delivers higher value than their untrained counterpart. Given the nature of the role, a trained 2iC working in tandem with an ambitious First-in-Command can expect a 6X impact.

2iC Chain

In a 2iC Chain, two or more Seconds-in-Command are linked together with a First-in-Command. A chain of 2iCs has an even more powerful effect than a single 2iC, creating the potential for a 10X impact (Figure 3).

I have had the privilege of being part of multiple 2iC chains. The results have been nothing short of

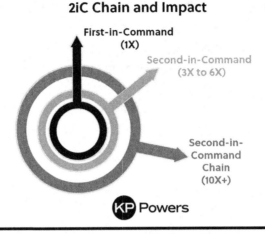

Figure 3   Second-in-Command (2iC) Chain and Impact.

phenomenal—and among the best experiences of my profes-sional life. The following are two examples:

- **Middle Circle**: I held a senior leadership position as the 2iC to the president while a member of my team served as a 2iC to me, creating a multiplying effect. The three of us combined accomplished phenomenal results.
- **Outer Circle**: I served as a 2iC to the 2iC to the presi-dent. Being the last link in a 2iC chain gave me a new perspective on the 2iC chain and its importance. Acting as a 2iC to another 2iC creates incredible momentum for accomplishing big goals with passion.

Bringing Value to Your Organization with 2iCs and 2iC Chains

The Second-in-Command, First in Excellence framework consists of four phases, each containing three sections, as shown in Figure 4. The journey of a 2iC is an infinity loop of learning in that the knowledge gained in each phase is

Figure 4 2iC Excellence Framework.

brought to bear in all the other phases. After completing the loop once, the 2iC is more prepared to complete the loop again, with the advantage of having the knowledge and experience from the previous iteration.

Ultimately, the 2iC is able to move through the loop faster and faster each time, with greater ease, precision, and success. The more times that a 2iC is able to complete the loop, the more prepared they are to manage any crises that arise because they've become more efficient at moving through each of the four phases and 12 stages.

Book Structure

This book is divided into five parts, one for each phase in the 2iC Excellence Framework shown in Figure 4, plus a part on blazing new trails.

- Phase A—Preparation focuses on the importance of looking ahead, embracing obsessive planning, and developing a financial strategy.
- Phase B—Building on the knowledge gained from Stage A, the book moves into Communication, which covers information gathering, the importance of overcommunicating, and managing cross-functional teams.
- Phase C—Empathy has become a hallmark quality for respected leaders. As such, it is the focus of Stage C, which explores compassionate ambition, explains why nothing good ever came from being too nice, and reveals the value of engaging with the curmudgeons.
- Phase D—Quality completes the infinity loop by explaining why you should always trust but verify, crosscheck exhaustively, and protect your #1.

• Blazing New Trails—This part of the book addresses the inevitable crises at organizations by utilizing the 2iC Excellence Framework to tackle emergency planning. Additionally, for organizations that want to achieve full maximum impact with 2iCs, I lay out the process for identifying and creating Second-in-Command chains in your organization.

Take Action—Progress Over Perfection

For ambitious leaders who want to achieve phenomenal success, this Stage ends with some action steps to engage your team in a Second-in-Command conversation.

1. How could your organization benefit from having 2iCs, not just at the top for the most senior leaders (as important as that is) but at all decision-maker levels?
2. Who are the 2iCs at your organization? Does your organization have any 2iC chains? How do 2iC chains' achievements compare to those of a single 2iC or a leader without a 2iC? If your organization has no 2iC chains, what kind of results might be achieved with a chain?
3. What is the next project that you (as an ambitious leader) can apply this framework too?
4. Ask your leadership team to read this Stage. If time permits, read or skim the remainder of the book, then engage in a team discussion about 2iCs at your organization.
   a. How could your organization benefit from having 2iCs?
   b. Which areas in the organization could most benefit from 2iCs and 2iC chains?
   c. What phenomenal successes could you (as an ambitious leader) achieve with a 2iC?

PHASE A

PREPARATION

The first of the four phases in the 2iC Excellence Framework is Preparation, which includes three stages:

1. Seeing a Few Steps Ahead
2. Planning Obsessively
3. Efficient Financial Strategy

DOI: 10.4324/9781003382003-2

Stage 1

Seeing a Few Steps Ahead

You are driving on the expressway in a fair amount of traffic. The signs are there: Lane Ends, Merge Left. Everyone on the road can see the signs. Yet the driver in front of you looks to be ignoring them and riding the lane out until the bitter end. What will the driver do at that point? Change lanes quickly? Go off the road?

Why isn't this driver paying attention? What are they thinking?

You're seeing all this from behind and know that the other driver should have put on their blinker a while ago (but didn't). You understand that this car will be coming into your lane at some point. It must—where else will it go when the other lane runs out?

Being forced to either speed up or slow down very quickly is less than ideal. There are more strategic options, such as getting in another lane, speeding up or slowing down more gradually, taking another route with less traffic, and so forth.

In the scenario above, your perspective is analogous to that of a Second-in-Command. 2iCs see disconnects and opportunities a few steps ahead of everyone else. They are constantly looking ahead to ward off problems and identify strategic opportunities.

Seeing a few steps ahead is the first Stage in the 2iC Excellence Framework because foresight is the "mother" of all 2iC skills. For example, without knowing the issues that lie ahead, you won't be able to decipher which things should get your more immediate attention and those that can and should wait or need some more thought.

Each Stage builds on the other. Without being able to see a few steps ahead, you are simply guessing what you should be obsessively planning (Stage 2). You can't really do any of the other stages without it, but if you can anticipate what might happen, you can plan obsessively in response. Thus, seeing a few steps ahead is Stage 1 in the 2iC Excellence Framework (Figure 5).

Seeing a Few Steps Ahead: What It Means in Action

Seeing a few steps ahead means playing out in your mind how a situation will unfold. Many people do this in games. Take chess or Scrabble: Before making a move or putting down tiles to form a word, a strategic player will consider what their opponent might do in response, anticipating future plays based on different permutations.

This type of thinking is much like a decision tree. As shown in Figure 6, a decision tree presents many different permutations and combinations for events. At first glance, the decision options can be overwhelming. That's why many people get stuck in the decision tree rather than getting started.

It typically is worthwhile to play out options for only a few branches of a decision tree. Exploring every possibility is

Figure 5   2iC Excellence Framework—Seeing a Few Steps Ahead—Stage 1.

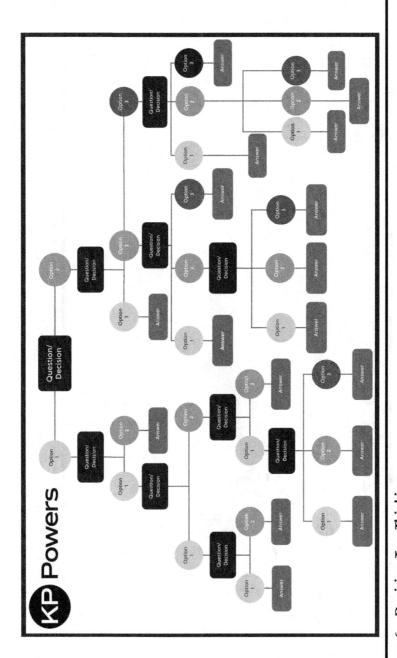

Figure 6   Decision-Tree Thinking.

time-consuming and usually results in making a move much too late, defeating the very purpose of seeing a few steps ahead.

The Value of Seeing Ahead

Why would anyone want to look ahead? What value is there in looking down the road rather than thinking more about the present? Among the most significant returns are time and cost savings.

Looking ahead to anticipate what might happen is a form of planning. Of course, the main idea behind planning is that if you plan for something, you are focused on a goal. As a result, you increase the likelihood of achieving your goal rather than hoping that things will magically work out.

Planning vs. Success

A study in which over 500 small business leaders were interviewed revealed that only 5% had accomplished all of their goals in the preceding 12 months (Jordan, 2020). This statistic isn't that surprising because leaders should be setting reach goals that they start chipping away at, but may not necessarily accomplish in just one year. Rather, it may take multiple years to achieve a goal.

Perhaps the goal is achieved the following year instead. The same study (Jordan, 2020) found that "nearly 65% of small business owners reported meeting more than half of their objectives in the past twelve months." That number seems low given the amount of time, effort, and energy businesses put into setting goals and aligning resources to achieve those goals, including the money spent on implementing initiatives.

Reading those statistics, one might think, "Well, those are small businesses with only a few people, so they don't do formal planning." Yet the Small Business Administration (SBA) "defines small business by firm revenue (ranging from $1 million to over $40 million) and by employment (from 100 to over 1,500 employees)" (Hait, 2021)—not the mom-and-pop outfits that might spring to mind. So there are many businesses that fall into the definition of a "small business" but the average person does not think of it as a small business.

Time, Money, and Reputation Saved by Seeing Ahead

By looking a few steps ahead, one can head off problems that might lead to wasted time and/or money. Consider this example:

A group of six to eight executives from a Fortune 500 company was conducting in-person visits with clients. Considerable logistical planning went into each visit, with each location and client having unique circumstances, such as start and end times. On the second to last visit, the administrative coordinator learned that the client meeting would end at 4:30 rather than 4:00. The agenda was promptly updated.

The 2iC in the group, who had developed a habit of looking ahead, was preparing for the trip and noticed that he would have only 45 minutes to make his flight after the visit. After reviewing the meeting materials, he identified the new end time as the issue. Unfortunately, not everyone in the group had gotten word of the change. The 2iC realized this and alerted all those traveling by plane that they might need to reschedule their flight. Had he not looked ahead, the executives would have had to make a choice on site in front of the client: Leave the meeting early (which is bad form) to make their flight or miss the flight, which would have resulted in additional overnight and airfare costs. In this case, the 2iC saved valuable time with the client, kept travel costs as budgeted, and spared his group from an embarrassing situation.

Benefits of Seeing Ahead

It Feels Good to Be Prepared and Get It Right

There are days when everything seems to fall into place. You hit every green light on the way to work and step in line at the grocery store checkout just before the rush. 2iCs feel this way all the time on the job, except that it doesn't happen by chance; it happens because they are always looking ahead.

2iCs look ahead, while others look at what is in front of them. Looking ahead gives 2iCs time to gear up to overcome obstacles rather than being surprised or stifled by them. This alleviates stress and anxiety and boosts confidence for upcoming tasks.

Staying Ahead Is Better Than Catching Up

Many employees are constantly trying to catch up, cleaning up problems resulting from not looking ahead. It's a vicious circle—you can't organize your thoughts for the meeting you're driving to because you forgot to fill up your tank the night before and now have to go out of your way to find a gas station. The next thing you know, you're speeding to make up lost time. Because you're in such a rush, you miss your turn and have to double back. You end up being late for the meeting and playing catch-up to figure out what every-one's talking about instead of participating fully in the discussion. The entire experience is hugely stressful.

2iCs rarely find themselves in such situations. On the rare occasion that they spend any time in the rearview mirror, they become so uncomfortable that they file away the lessons learned and determine never to repeat the same mistakes again.

Project Hindsight

For example, on any large project, it is customary to have subject matter experts sign off that they have reviewed all materials for compliance with their department's standards. I once experienced some time in the rearview mirror while managing a major data project that involved a large committee. It was necessary to overcommunicate (a practice discussed later in this book) throughout the project, which lasted more than six months. The committee met weekly to examine data and project requirements. Each member's verbal approval was obtained at significant milestones. A final "high-level" review was the last step of the project.

Imagine my surprise when a committee member who had actively participated in the weekly meetings threw a giant wrench into the final review by revealing a critical requirement that he had never disclosed. Six months of work were abruptly upended. Making a substantial change to the deliverable at such a late date, especially when the rest of the committee would not have a chance to review the additional requirement to assess its other downstream effects, would cause significant problems. This often includes wrong information being provided because sufficient time isn't available to go through normal development and review processes.

I spent time in the rearview mirror cleaning up the mess so the deliverable could be sent on-time to avoid missing a federal deadline. I dislike spending my time that way—it's stressful and time-consuming. But the work needs to be done, and slogging through it serves as a valuable lesson to avoid the same set of circumstances in the future.

In this case, I first worked with the developers to get the new requirement into the code as quickly as possible. Next, I worked one-on-one with the various committee members to review the changes so they could each perform their final review and provide their sign-off. This was all on top of my other already scheduled projects and responsibilities.

Once the crisis had passed, I spent considerable time trying to understand where I'd gone wrong. I wasn't going to let the same thing ever happen again. While a project post-mortem is instructive for avoiding mistakes in the future, it is also important to limit how much time is spent rehashing the past. I now require written sign-off on major projects, not just verbal approval. If written sign-off had been required on the project in question, the committee member would have taken his approval more seriously.

Take Action—Progress Over Perfection

Questions for Reflection and Discussion

1. What are your decision-making processes and how do you play out actions in your head?
2. How do you visualize or play out a situation before taking action?
3. Think back on a work project that didn't go as well as it could have. Were there opportunities to see ahead and influence the outcome? If so, what were they? What could you have done?
4. How do you avoid "surprises" that are not in the scope of the project?
5. What are three strategies you currently use to "see ahead?" How often do you utilize them? Can you use them more? How about today?

Stage 2

Planning Obsessively

As a 2iC, you likely have had to travel for business. Needless to say, it's not the same as traveling for fun. Among the many differences, traveling for business is tied to an agenda with specific places to be at exact times. Traveling for pleasure is generally more fluid, with fewer events requiring punctuality (e.g., transportation).

Of course, both types of travel require packing. Forgetting something for your business trip can range from being a minor inconvenience to a huge problem. For example, forgetting your preferred shampoo isn't so bad. You might dislike the hotel-supplied shampoo, but it will get the job done if you absolutely must wash your hair. If this were a fun travel trip, you might go to a store and buy some shampoo, but it's a work trip, so you're too pressed for time to do that.

More disastrous would be forgetting dress pants or your computer charger. There aren't any substitutions or quick fixes for those. With work travel, there is so little wiggle room that it is imperative to get things right. And while most people do get the big stuff right, 2iCs get *everything* right, taking planning to a whole other level.

DOI: 10.4324/9781003382003-4

Here's a quick example before we dig into Planning Obsessively:

On one of my recent business trips, a meeting participant was drinking hot water. The person sitting next to her remarked, "Just hot water?" She responded that there was no green tea available. Overhearing this, I pulled some green tea bags out of my briefcase and offered her one. Both she and the other person were stunned. "You just walk around with green tea in your bag?" she asked. I said, "Yes, yes I do." Since most places only serve coffee in meetings and coffee disagrees with me, I've learned to carry a stack of green tea bags with me because I almost always can find water and a microwave in a pinch. That's being obsessively prepared. In this particular instance, it allowed me to form a personal connection with someone I'd never met before and also reinforced my reputation as a next-level planner with the other person (whom I knew already).

As such, Planning Obsessively is the second Stage of the 2iC Excellence Framework (Figure 7).

Planning Obsessively: What It Means in Action

To prepare for something—an event, a test, a meeting—indicates that you have thought about the knowns and likely variables involved and planned accordingly. However, to be obsessively prepared is to take planning to an advanced professional level.

The word "obsessive" has negative connotations, but I think of Planning Obsessively as a continuous loop of review and evaluation that occurs until the event or project concludes. Because circumstances evolve—the weather turns; a flight gets canceled; someone gets sick—it is important to constantly assess whether any changes have taken place and if so how they might impact the project or goal.

Figure 7   2iC Excellence Framework—Planning Obsessively—Stage 2.

The Value of Planning Obsessively

There are multiple types of currency, the most obvious being money. Time is another. When you save both time and money, returns are even greater than simple cost savings.

Saving time and money doesn't happen by accident. It isn't even guaranteed with planning. However, the odds of saving time and money increase exponentially with Planning Obsessively. Planning Obsessively ratchets good up to great. "Great managers know where we are going, and all the risks involved in getting there. Their role is to coach their team through the obstacles and get them to the other side" (Gaborit, 2022).

Planning, Preparation, and Planning Obsessively

There is a difference between planning, preparation, and Planning Obsessively. To discuss the differences, I first begin with planning avoidance—the counterpoint to planning—to describe planning before moving on to the advantage of preparation and planning obsessively (Figure 8).

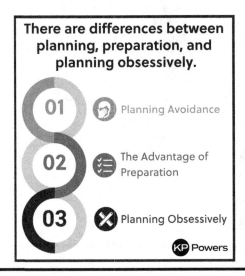

Figure 8 **Difference between Planning, Preparation, and Planning Obsessively.**

Planning Avoidance

Planning is thinking about a future event and outlining the steps to make it happen. The end goal is a successful event. Many think planning is boring. They feel that planning is limiting and stifles creativity. As a result, some will say, "Well, I've never really been a good planner" as a way to avoid planning or as a license to "wing it." Instead of rejecting all planning, they would do well to explore higher levels of planning, such as preparation and Planning Obsessively. Self-proclaimed non-planners might find that they really enjoy the preparation.

The Advantage of Preparation

Preparation still means having the goal in mind but recognizes that multiple detours or unanticipated issues can arise on the way to achieving that goal. Consequently, plans are conceived for multiple scenarios, not just one ideal scenario.

Planning Obsessively: A Key Skill for 2iCs

Taking preparation to the obsessive level increases the odds of achieving great success. Seconds-in-Command don't just prepare; they review their preparations over and over again throughout the journey to the end goal, looking for any speed-bumps, roadblocks, necessary changes, or new information.

Planning Obsessively allows 2iCs to remove a lot of anxiety from the entire process of working toward a goal. Firsts-in-Command and colleagues need never worry whether their organization will accomplish the goal because 2iCs are utilizing their Planning Obsessively superpower to recalibrate steps along the way to ensure success. No one has to wonder whether or not the project will meet the First-in-Command's expectations. Such sources of anxiety can slow the organization down.

The responsibility of the Second-in-Command is to identify potential issues ahead of time (Stage 1), obsessively prepare for them, and make sure that adjustments are being made throughout the process to ensure success. Planning Obsessively is about taking the time upfront to identify and plan for unexpected twists in the road, ensuring that neither you nor anyone else in your organization will have to worry about bad outcomes.

Benefits of Planning Obsessively

It Feels Great to Be Prepared

It feels great to be prepared—really great. Anyone who has studied hard for a test and experienced the feeling of having mastered the content knows what it's like—that certainty that you're going to get an A. Imagine this then: You have worked hard to prepare for an important event, and everything not only goes according to plan but turns out even better than anyone (except maybe you) expected. Everything seems to run flawlessly (even though there might be a few hiccups that you know about but no one else sees).

I've coordinated multiple large professional and travel events, and all of my Planning Obsessively paid off when they unfolded in ways that exceeded expectations for attendees and participants alike. Stellar event evaluations and personal words of thanks, both verbal and written, provided further proof of the value of Planning Obsessively.

Preparation Skills Have Benefits Beyond the Workplace

When preparing for a vacation, you likely do research up front to find restaurants that serve the kind of food you like or learn about the different activities that you might be interested in doing depending on the weather and your level of energy on a particular day.

All the effort put into knowing what possibilities are available to you pays off when you get to your destination and can easily pivot from going on a hike to spending the day at the beach. Maybe you've investigated the dining options so well that if one restaurant is too busy or you don't feel like a particular cuisine that night, you have other choices for a fantastic meal at your fingertips.

It feels better to have done all that preparation and then have everything go smoothly on your vacation. In the end, all the time and effort you put in upfront was totally worth it because you get to enjoy your vacation that much more. You don't have to spend time poring over Yelp reviews instead of relaxing; you've already read them and know all the best places to go.

Making Mistakes Feels Crummy

Just as getting things right feels really good, making mistakes or forgetting to complete a task feels super crummy. It's also a waste of time, resources—including money because you end up having to pay more for some kind of expedited service. If you forget to submit your credit card payment on time, the company charges interest and a late fee. It's something that happens to just about everyone at one time or another, a simple oversight, but it still feels crummy and wastes money.

When a Second-in-Command makes a mistake or forgets to do something, it usually has a ripple effect because the role requires working with many people, especially in cross-functional teams (Stage 6). For example, forgetting to inform a workgroup that a deadline has been moved up leaves the entire group scrambling once they hear the news. The impact on others can be significant and potentially damage trust.

2iCs learn very quickly that there is great value in putting in a little extra time to look ahead (Stage 1) and overcommunicate (Stage 5).

Take Action—Progress Over Perfection

Questions for Reflection and Discussion

1. How has planning obsessively, intensely helped you achieve success?
2. Recall a time when you spent the time to obsessively prepare. What were the results? What was successful because of the planning obsessively? How did you feel about the results afterward?
3. What is the difference between being prepared and planning obsessively to you?
4. What is the cost of mistakes, poor communication, and lost time in your organization?
5. How do you feel when you make a mistake or forget to do something due to a lack of preparing or planning obsessively?

Stage 3

Efficient Financial Strategy

Even the best ideas still need to be financially viable. Better to know the true costs so the project can have a chance of success ... or sunset it because it was doomed for failure.

Whether you dream of retiring or simply having more time and money to do the things you want to do, you need to have a financial strategy to achieve, or get as close as possible to, financial independence. For some, retirement sounds like a wonderful permanent vacation; for others, it sounds terrible. Why would they want to stop doing work that they love at the early age of 67, with oodles of knowledge gained and no one to share it with? That's why many people have come to see beyond the binary choice of either retiring or not retiring.

Enter financial independence and its different schools of thought (e.g., coasting to financial independence and FIRE, which stands for "financial independence, retire early"). This option offers a blended life of working and doing "retirement activities" such as traveling, spending more time with family and friends, trying new hobbies, and so forth,

DOI: 10.4324/9781003382003-5

long before age 67. It requires a willingness to take a less beaten path but promises aspects of a lifestyle formerly reserved only for retirees.

Whether you gravitate toward traditional retirement or are interested in financial independence models, you need to develop an efficient financial strategy. The more involved and creative you can be with that strategy, the more options you will have in achieving your goals. The same is true for ambitious leaders in the workplace, which is why Developing an Efficient Financial Strategy is Stage 3 in the 2iC Excellence Framework (Figure 9).

Developing an efficient financial strategy is part of Phase A (Preparation) because the process provides 2iCs with key information to distinguish real problems from foot dragging and keep projects moving forward. Efficient Financial Strategy is early on in the 2iC Excellence Framework because it is critical to have viable finances for the effort; otherwise, energy spent on Stages 4 through 12 would be wasted.

Developing an Efficient Financial Strategy: What It Means in Action

Gone are the days when financial planning was the sole responsibility of one office or division. Financial literacy used to be a differentiator for ambitious leaders. Now that all leaders need a solid understanding of finances, those wishing to stand out must level up their financial acumen.

This means going beyond having a general financial strategy (e.g., sell a great product or service and money will come) to having an *efficient* financial strategy in which deliberate attention is paid to maximizing resources such that there is no waste and no financial surprises arise. In other words, the financial strategy receives just as much attention as the goal or project itself.

Figure 9 2iC Excellence Framework—Efficient Financial Strategy—Stage 3.

Leading the Development of an Efficient Financial Strategy

Someone needs to take the lead on creating an efficient financial strategy. While it is expected that there will be multiple reviewers, one person still has to be in charge. There are two options: the project creator or someone in the budgeting/finance department. Neither is ideal. However, the idea creator knows—and cares—more about their idea than anyone else in the entire organization. More leaders need to ramp up their financial expertise so they are qualified to take charge when it's their idea that needs a strategy; some are opting to do so as the new differentiator to get their ideas heard and implemented.

Some leaders tell (or whisper to) me that they are not good at finance. So they don't do it. They don't want to show their shortcomings. Well, they're showing their shortcomings by not diving into financial strategy. Rest assured that the skills required to develop a financial strategy—even an efficient financial strategy—are well within the grasp of any ambitious leader.

The First Iteration of an Efficient Financial Strategy Isn't Perfect

One of the things that many non-finance people don't know is that the first iteration of a financial strategy doesn't have to be perfect—and can't be. No one else has looked at it to provide insights from a different vantage point. Changes resulting from their feedback will make the financial strategy even more efficient. Think of the first iteration as a starting offer and know there will be a few rounds of negotiation.

An efficient financial strategy begins with two familiar concepts—revenues and expenses. To transform a financial strategy into an efficient financial strategy, the models and tables need to provide some details. That does not mean the document has to be long. In fact, the efficient financial strategy models that I create with clients are one page—no one wants to look at more than that initially.

Agree on the Floor of Revenues

A detailed revenues section will note the assumptions on which the revenue forecast is based. This allows readers to judge whether you are optimistic or conservative in your numbers. For example, if the industry standard for repeat customers is 60% within one year and the efficient financial strategy is based on 55%, readers can see that some wiggle room has been built. We can disagree on the figure of 55%. Some may think it should be 56%; others, 62%. But if we can agree that 55% is a reasonable floor, then we can move on to the next assumption.

Estimate Slightly Higher for Expenses

It's on the expense side that the idea creator's subject matter expertise is required so that all project needs are included. For example, the idea creator knows how much marketing will need to be done in year one versus year three or the specialized software or equipment that will be critical to the success of the project by differentiating the product or service from competitors. Again, we can disagree on the exact numbers, but having reasonable (preferably slightly higher than expected) estimates is the goal—not perfection.

Net Profits That Cause Movement

Add up the revenues. Add up the expenses. Subtract expenses from the revenues to arrive at the net profit or loss. Having a profit of $1 doesn't offer much of a buffer for error. What if costs increase? Even though $1 is a profit, it isn't a compelling profit that will motivate others to take the risk of approving the project.

All is not lost. Look to see where assumptions can be reasonably adjusted or expenses might be reduced. For example, could a full-time employee be added in year three after more steady revenues come in? Revisit and tweak each line until the financial strategy reaches maximum efficiency.

The Value of Having an Efficient Financial Strategy

Having a financial strategy is really about having enough money to devote to top-level priorities. It can be super, super frustrating when an organization funds items that are well known to be less important—items that are not connected or at least don't appear to be connected with established priorities. A good financial strategy will guard against the diversion of funding to lower-level priorities.

A more advanced financial strategy will also allow for unanticipated or emergency issues. However, more than half of businesses are not connecting the dots between their budget and their strategic plans (Platinum Group, 2020). Because their budget isn't aligned with known priorities, let alone any problems that might crop up, they are setting themselves up for challenges before the fiscal year has even begun.

Priority Mismatches Lead to Confusion and Avoidance

When low priorities are funded at the expense of high priorities after months of budget meetings and the development of a financial strategy, much confusion results. This leads many people to think that finance is hard because they literally don't understand how these financial decisions were made. It isn't that finance is hard. Decisions influenced by emotion and/or bad information are often the culprit.

People who think finance is hard often end up avoiding it. They adopt a philosophy of spending now and figuring it out later (and/or using credit). Most people know they don't have enough money for everything they want. The truth is that no one has enough money for everything they want.

However, there is a big difference between having enough money for everything you want and having enough money to meet your current priorities and move toward your goals.

It isn't really about having enough money. It's about taking the money you have and routing it to your priorities. For example, some people will forgo taking a vacation for a year or two in order to make a larger down-payment on a house or pay for graduate school.

The 2iC's Role in Financial Strategy

While finance can seem intimidating, especially with all of the jargon, the key is to keep it simple and in layperson's terms. You don't need to be a chief financial officer to get involved in finance and budgeting. In fact, 2iCs that are courageous enough to dive into money matters have a skill that finance professionals don't have—they keep it simple. 2iCs explain things in commonly understood language, which those who sweat the finance stuff appreciate.

As a Second-in-Command, you do not need to be a finance expert. A 2iC's differentiator is understanding finance at a high level and being able to communicate general revenues and general expenses—"Here's how much money this project is going to cost" (rough estimates) and "Here's how much money the project will bring in based on X, Y, and Z assumptions." Remember, if you don't understand the financial quagmires the experts are talking about, other non-experts won't either.

Seconds-in-Command need to demonstrate that the financial strategy covers the key components of the project and that the numbers therein are neither overly optimistic nor overly restrictive.

Keeping the Ball Rolling

The goal is to make decision-makers more comfortable with taking the time to fully flesh out the project and get the finance gurus to add their expertise and patina. If the decision-makers understand the finances at a level that really resonates with them (in a way that jargon likely won't), the project will have a higher probability of moving forward. It is the job of the 2iC to make that happen. One of the most important parts of having a financial strategy is articulating the specific value of what the organization is spending money on. Ideally, multiple leaders can communicate the financial strategy to their teams in their own words, thus creating advocacy for the project.

The 2iC's goal is to move the project forward. Determining budget and affordability is vital to forward momentum. Once the major financial components are figured out, the finance experts can come in for the final patina. The 2iC is like a surgeon performing the most complex part of a medical procedure. It takes an entire team in the operating room for the surgery to be completed. There is still important work for skilled medical professionals to do after the surgeon has set the patient on the path to improved health. Similarly, the 2iC can turn to capable, qualified individuals to add the necessary level of detail to get the financials "cleaned up."

Transparent Financial Strategies Make Information Accessible

If the organization has a financial strategy, folks can have trade-off conversations about priorities. Everyone always thinks that their initiative is the most important. As already stated, it is essential that the financial components be clearly articulated in layperson's terms: How much is there to spend? How much can you move around? What are the start-up costs? Is there enough money for the project to be successful?

If this information is not provided, it will be impossible to rank priorities. How will decision-makers know what the trade-offs are? Without clear and easy-to-understand financial information on each project, people will not understand why some projects are funded, leading to frustration and siloed departments within an organization. Conversely, if the financial strategy and high-level financials for projects are laid out transparently to all those affected, productive conversations and trust will ensue.

Timing Is Everything

Seconds-in-Command must always keep in mind the importance of timing. One of the things that I love about financial strategies is that the fiscal year ends and a new one begins—every year! It's almost like getting a "do-over."

If your idea didn't resonate enough with decision-makers to get funded last year, you can pitch it again for the next fiscal year. Being a successful 2iC is very much about finding the right time to pitch a project to a partner or endorser. For example, sometimes end-of-year money is available and needs to be spent.

In other cases, it is easier to get positive movement at the beginning of the year, when money might be more readily available. People might be more receptive to hearing your ideas and putting them on the docket to be funded.

As a project gets closer to completion, having a financial strategy allows you to know and articulate the amount spent versus allocated. There are key meetings during the year where this information becomes critical to communicate and advocate for additional funding. You can communicate to your First-in-Command, investment committee, or whoever is making the financial decisions the next-level impact that can be achieved with additional funding.

For example, "We achieved X, Y, and Z with last year's funding and have enough evidence to show that an additional investment of this amount would double the impact for the organization." Again, transparency helps to communicate value. Even if you need to go ask for more money or spent more than anticipated, you have the reasoning behind it.

Sharing an efficient financial strategy allows you to communicate information about a project in a way that can effect change and get the right priorities accomplished with intention as opposed to spending freely and hoping that you fall within budget by the end of the year or being afraid to go back and ask for more because you got only so much at the beginning of the year. If you can track spending and know the value that you're targeting, then you'll most likely be able to get more investment where and when you want it.

Benefits of Efficient Financial Strategies

The Truth Is the Truth

Having developed hundreds of efficient financial strategies with clients and colleagues, I can attest that one of two amazing things happens as a result (Figure 10): (1) the project is implemented and is more structurally sound because it is

Efficient Financial Strategy

Project is implemented, is structurally sound, and adequately funded.

Obtain a better understanding of why the project wasn't approved.

Inefficient Financial Strategy Re-Work

See the fatal flaw from the perspective of other leaders.

Address the problems and deficiencies with modifications so that it becomes an Efficient Financial Strategy.

Shift focus to a new project with greater viability.

KP Powers

Figure 10   Efficient and Inefficient Financial Strategy Rework.

adequately funded or (2) idea creators obtain a much better understanding of why their project hasn't been approved. They begin to see the fatal flaw from the perspective of other leaders. The idea creator then either addresses the problems and deficiencies with modifications to make the project work (making the project better than initially conceptualized) or shifts their focus to a new project with greater viability. This time around, the idea creator is more knowledgeable about the process and is able to draft an efficient financial strategy on their own.

Facing the truth—including hard financial truths—sooner rather than later leaves more time to course correct. As LeAnn McGowan, Vice President of Business Intelligence at TruConnect, notes,

> Seconds-in-Command need to feel comfortable and empowered to speak the truth. For many people, they don't want to face the facts now for fear of ramifications or pushback; they'll face the facts later. Rather, I say: Let's face the facts around critical business decisions now. And then let's not be disappointed or surprised later when the outcome is not what we expected.

It Should Be Criminal to Delay a Financially Viable Project

The late General Colin Powell's remark that "Bad news is not like wine; it doesn't get better with age" comes to mind. If the project isn't financially viable, avoiding finances won't make it any more possible.

If the project is or could be financially viable with some modifications, every day those modifications are postponed is money lost. These are among the most frustrating situations for me. The hard work of developing a financially viable idea has been done. The finish line is in sight and just needs to be crossed!

Of course, irrelevant excuses—"We don't have the start-up funds for it" or "It isn't the right time"— are typically given as reasons for not moving forward with a great idea that is a financial no-brainer. As frustrating as those comments might be, it is important to note the roadblocks that are being put up so that you can address them and obtain the necessary approvals. I'll talk more about listening to what is said and not said in the Obvious and Hidden Information Gathering (Stage 4) section. I don't give up easily.

The Opportunities Don't Get Better Than This One

As an example from my 2iC experience, I once was part of a proposal to offer a new service. It was well known in the organization that I not only enjoyed the efficient financial strategy process but also had a knack for it. Often I can articulate the financial benefits in a compelling way in only one or two meetings with the idea creator. While I have not had formal finance training, I've been doing maximum money-moving gymnastics and derivatives in my head for as long as I can remember. You could say that I've been calculating efficiencies since my mother caught me one night counting the money in my piggy bank. (I said I couldn't sleep until I'd finished.)

When the idea to offer a new service came up with a colleague, I quickly began doing the math in my head. I raced to my efficient financial strategy templates to enter the inputs because I was excited to see the net profits. I prefer (and recommend) doing three-year models. Year 1 usually has some larger and/or one-time expenses, and the numbers are more compelling and reflective of longer-term expectations by year 3.

The net profits were better than expected. I showed my colleague. We made some tweaks and put together the proposal content that was in our heads to accompany the finances. The whole proposal needed to be delivered to leadership as a package, not piecemeal. This proposal was about as no-brainer as it gets. It came as a great shock that the CEO sat on it. He didn't say yes or no, he just sat on it!

No decision is still a decision, though. My colleague and I began to discuss and piece together the reasons for the delay. I wanted to know what the roadblocks were so that we could get to work removing them.

Having been through the 2iC infinity loop thousands of times, I quickly moved into the communication and empathy phases detailed later in this book. Using the 2iC Excellence Framework, I was able to clear the way for the project to move forward. The roadblocks in question did not involve money.

We would later learn that there was a hidden issue. The CEO didn't understand how the offering fit with the existing offerings. He couldn't connect the dots. And if he couldn't immediately see it, how were others expected to see the connection?

After unearthing this one piece of hidden information, I suspected there were more pieces to discover too. This couldn't be the only roadblock. However, moving forward in the 2iC Excellence Framework to the next Stage (Obvious and Hidden Information Gathering) was the next step.

Take Action—Progress Over Perfection

Questions for Reflection and Discussion

1. What has been the most challenging part of developing an efficient financial strategy?
2. What are some ways that you can connect the dots between projects and budgeting? Who can you network within the organization? What projects or committees can you work on or participate in to learn more about financials?
3. To what degree does developing an efficient financial strategy contribute to the success of projects at your organization?
4. Combine the skills of seeing ahead and planning obsessively. How can you use those skills to develop an efficient financial strategy that enables success such that you can move to stage 4?
5. There is never enough money for everything; how do you utilize your role as a 2iC to ensure that the focus, including finances, is on priority projects that deliver value?

PHASE B

COMMUNICATION

The majority of a 2iC's job is to get others who do not functionally report to them to complete work, which is why communication is the second of the four phases of the 2iC Excellence Framework. Phase B: Communication includes three stages:

4. Obvious and Hidden Information Gathering
5. Overcommunicating
6. Managing Cross-Functional Teams

DOI: 10.4324/9781003382003-6

Stage 4

Obvious and Hidden Information Gathering

Seconds-in-Command must obtain information throughout the organization to stay ahead of the game and solve problems. As a result, 2iCs need to continually leverage existing relationships and also build new relationships well beyond their immediate team, department, or even division. Every 2iC interviewed for this book talked about how important it was for them to build relationships and establish trust in order to fulfill their duties, including information gathering.

Tiffany Paine-Cirrincione, Director of Development and Communications at St. Joseph's Neighborhood Center, shared,

> As a cancer survivor, I often say, 'if they can't find it, I can't fight it.' And it's the same thing with relationships and with organizational structures. If the important things are going unsaid because people don't have the trust or are afraid to say them, then we've all failed. It is important for both the first and second in commands to have joint trust to have difficult conversations for forward progress.

DOI: 10.4324/9781003382003-7

The huge increase in remote and hybrid work caused by the Covid pandemic has changed the way employees obtain information from colleagues. Hallway chats and pre- and post-meeting conversations that took place in person were invaluable sources of information that have disappeared for organizations that haven't had a 100% return to the office. Everyone has had to develop new communication pathways to gather the information needed to do their work. This has been especially impactful for 2iCs given their heavy reliance on information, which requires relationships and trust. While virtual interactions are better than nothing, they are no replacement for face-to-face contact.

Many people who were working remotely before the pandemic now feel a greater connection to their colleagues because remote workers are no longer outliers. In fast-paced organizations where relationships are the gateway to golden nuggets of information, virtual relationship building is too slow to keep up. However, a combination of in-person and virtual relationship building could be the type of skill differentiator that takes a 2iC to new levels. As such, Obvious and Hidden Information Gathering is Stage 4 of the 2iC Excellence Framework (Figure 11).

Obvious and Hidden Information Gathering: What It Means in Action

In order to be a few steps ahead of current events, one needs to gather information. Obvious information—comments and observations that people are willing to share or existing reports—is easily obtained. It is much harder and requires more skill to gather hidden information—the things that people are *not* saying, either because they don't want to share what they know out loud or because they aren't even aware enough that there is an issue to be able to articulate it. Additionally, more information seems to be unintentionally hidden or misunderstood with virtual meetings.

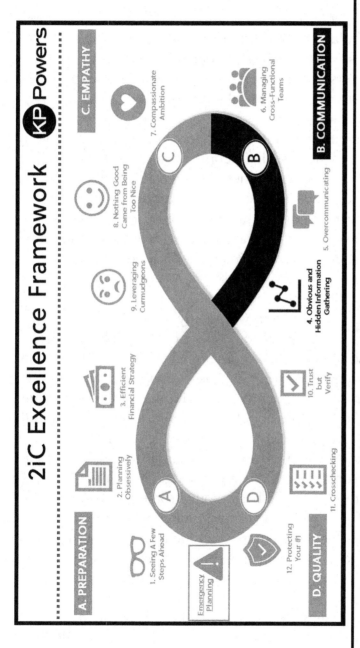

Figure 11 2iC Excellence Framework—Obvious & Hidden Information Gathering—Stage 4.

Direct Diplomacy

My 2iC experience with one particular client illustrates obvious and hidden information gathering in a hybrid environment. This was before the pandemic, and I was the outlier as the only person working remotely; everyone else involved in the project was on-site. Further complicating matters, all communications were via email or phone. as the video meeting culture and technology were not yet ubiquitous, I did not have the benefit of seeing people's faces, and they had no opportunity to see me either. We were just lines of text on a screen or disembodied voices to each other.

It seems odd now to think that we all agreed that we would be successful on the project with email and phone only. Even minimal video interaction to see each other's faces and facial expressions was absent. As a result, it was extremely difficult for me as a 2iC to gather obvious information; hidden information was nearly impossible!

And as an observer would suspect, the limited tools of communication presented other challenges too. The first to have a direct impact on the project arose quickly and right on cue when I was communicating with one of the organization's curmudgeons. (More about dealing with curmudgeons in the section on Stage 9; they can be valuable to a 2iC.) At the time, I didn't know the person was a curmudgeon. Sometimes a great person can look like a curmudgeon on a bad day, so it is better to assume the best about people and be on the lookout for more instances of curmudgeonly behavior.

Needing to make progress on the project, I began with the easiest-to-obtain information. This included requests for last year's report, prior emails, insights from subject matter experts, and the like. Even these obvious information requests were being met very slowly—definitely a yellow flag. I was keeping my red flag nearby as I was sure that I would be waving it soon.

Kind Collaborators to the Rescue

More time, emails, and phone calls passed. My attempts to obtain the hidden information were aided largely by Kind Collaborators, many of whom were grateful to have a fresh ear to vent to about the wrath of the curmudgeons. Since the Kind Collaborators were experienced in creating new trails around the curmudgeons, they were willing to offer guidance and shortcuts—confidentially, of course.

A few interactions with Kind Collaborators as well as the curmudgeon in which I posed thoughtful and strategic questions in a direct but diplomatic manner rendered enough information to understand the situation. Now that I had a clear picture of the obstacle course that I needed to navigate, I was able to leverage my 2iC skill set (described throughout this book) to reduce it to a bumpy path. It was thanks to these combined 2iC skills that the project was delivered to the project manager a few days ahead of schedule and with full transparency. While the project manager was not surprised by how the events unfolded, she did thank me for my direct diplomacy as she appreciated having specifics to address a larger issue relating to the curmudgeon.

Had I not pieced together all of the information points, including a lack of information (yes, a lack of information is telling as well), I would not have had the big picture view that allowed me to successfully navigate the obstacles to complete the project. The pieces of information weren't valuable individually, but collectively they formed a mosaic.

The Value of Obvious and Hidden Information Gathering

The amount of content available for reading and listening is overwhelming. As of May 2021, "Each day on Earth we generate

500 million tweets, 294 billion emails, 4 million gigabytes of Facebook data, 65 billion WhatsApp messages and 720,000 hours of new content added daily on YouTube" (Vopson, 2021).

It's virtually impossible to sift through all of the content that's out there to determine its usefulness in solving a given problem or meeting particular needs. As a result, Seconds-in-Command need to develop tactics for knowing where to go for actionable information.

During the interviews for this book, many 2iCs talked about their historical knowledge as a key resource for getting things done. Having been at their organization for a long period of time, they have been able to build relationships and trust and learn whom to go to for what.

As Angela Henderson, Chief Data Architect at Trivium BI, explains,

> You need to have the willingness to develop rela-tionships. As a Second-in-Command, much of your success comes from the relationships you've built. By working on projects together you build relation-ships in a more natural way. This leads to better communication flow that can feel open so that you can ask questions or ask for guidance. That's what really makes the relationship work.

While many employees have longevity at an organization, Seconds-in-Command use theirs to their distinct advantage. 2iCs can leverage their longevity because they have figured out who has information relevant to whichever topic they're working on. Knowing where to find these hidden pieces of information is like having access to a treasure map with the unwritten organizational chart that enables 2iCs to see and understand the pathways to information.

Obvious Information

Obvious information is, of course, obvious—say, the contents of an annual or recent project report that a supervisor, co-worker, or colleague points you to. Obvious information exists on the organization's website and intranet, in recent board and executive meeting materials, in quarterly reports, and so forth.

Hidden Information

The hidden information is more challenging and takes more of these combined 2iC skills to access. Part of being a successful 2iC is knowing how to navigate an organization to find information. It might not even be hidden, but you need to know whom to talk to.

Being aware of happenings across the organization, even if they are not currently and/or directly related to your 2iC work, can provide you with early indicators or background knowledge for future projects or challenges. This awareness, in combination with both unwritten and formal organizational charts, will allow you to determine the right person to go to for the right status update.

The Devil's in the Details

Anyone can look at a project status update to see the red, amber, and green indicators. However, to get a true under-standing of what's happening behind the scenes, the 2iC needs to talk to the person most closely connected to the piece of the project that the First-in-Command needs to know about. It's difficult for a First-in-Command to keep track of all the project details, which is why they need a Second-in-Command to handle the specifics.

The 2iC can be working with team members at the operational level in the trenches, getting access to the right folks to gather information that seems hidden to other outsiders. As a skilled 2iC, you know just whom to ask for the specifics necessary to provide the First-in-Command with a comprehensive update.

Benefits of Obvious and Hidden Information Gathering

Meeting Lovers

I can think of a few 2iCs who love meetings. Most people don't. At some point, we all have been in a meeting and thought to ourselves (or shared via instant message), "This meeting could have been an email."

When I really thought about why some people love meetings, I came to the conclusion that it's because they love discovering new hidden information. Hidden information has a way of revealing itself before a meeting through idle chit-chat, during a meeting through body language, or after a meeting through conversations. Of course, with the pandemic-era shift to hybrid and remote work, video meetings became the norm for many participants. While the pandemic has largely passed, hybrid habits have not.

Video meetings are now part of many organizations' culture. This has had a significant impact on communication, including obtaining hidden information. For example, while participants are typically encouraged to turn on their camera during video meetings, not everyone does so. Even for regular camera users, there are days or times of the day, such as very early in the morning, when a meeting participant may not be able to turn their camera on (e.g., family members are home and in the background, meeting begins at 7 a.m. Pacific Time, 10 a.m. Eastern time and you haven't gotten ready for the day yet, not feeling well, etc.).

Those Seconds-in-Command who once relied heavily on obtaining hidden information from in-person interactions have lost an important tool and found their skills diminished. As a result, they have had to recalibrate how they go about obtaining that hidden information, cultivating more regular one-on-one contact via email and turning to instant messaging for that real-time connection.

Answering the Question You Should Have Asked

I have a friend who is known in our circle for saying, "If I like you, I'll answer the question you should have asked. But if I don't like you, I'll just answer the question you asked, even though I know you'll be back for follow-up questions you should have really asked" (Figure 12). The point here is that it is

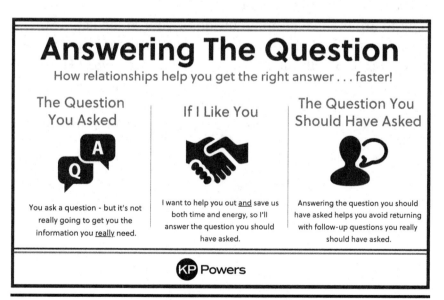

Figure 12   Answering the Question You Should Have Asked.

important as a Second-in-Command to hear the question that is really being asked and understand what the person is really after rather than just focusing on the actual words spoken. Additionally, the 2iC needs to ask the right questions to ensure that the request and pain-points can be appropriately addressed.

Take Action—Progress Over Perfection

Questions for Reflection and Discussion

1. What are two to three ways that you have been successful in gathering hidden information? How often do you use these strategies? Could you use them more and increase your project success and/or reduce speed bumps?
2. What historical knowledge has been most important to have as a 2iC?
3. What are some ways you can stay aware of what is going on across the organization?
4. Who are the five people outside of your immediate team that would be helpful to you as a 2iC? What is your relationship with them? Can you make it stronger? How?
5. What have you discovered about your organization that would surprise an outsider? How can you leverage this information to be a strength for the organization in your 2iC work?

Stage 5

Overcommunicating

One of the keys to being successful as a Second-in-Command is not just to communicate, but to overcommunicate. Communicate early, often, repetitively, and thoroughly. Communicating is expected; everyone needs to do it. Overcommunicating takes the skill to another level and is quite different than simply repeating yourself.

People often need to receive information multiple times and in different formats before it sinks in. Someone may interpret the message incorrectly the first time. In many cases, people hear what they want to hear, so it is important to repeat the information so that the intended message gets through to them.

If at First You Don't Succeed

For example, while serving as a 2iC, I came up with an idea that would have a significant and positive impact on customers. I was so excited about the possibilities that I quickly found time on a colleague's calendar to share my revelation

DOI: 10.4324/9781003382003-8

with her. I just knew she would love the idea and see its potential the same way I did.

After I shared the idea, she asked a question or two out of politeness and then changed the topic. That was it! She was done hearing about the idea. I thought that maybe she needed some time to digest it. In a couple of weeks, I saw her at a meeting and asked how the project was coming along. She gave me a blank stare, trying to recall what I was talking about. I've forgotten what she said, but it was something vague and a brush-off.

I wasn't giving up on this idea. I did some more research, thinking, and plotting. I made two more failed attempts at pitching the idea in different ways. Finally, after some changes in leadership and requests to approach customers differently, I made one last pitch. At long last, the idea resonated with my colleague. To my great shock, she acted as if she had never heard it before, as if we had not had multiple conversations about it.

I almost didn't bring the idea up that last time, but I believed in it so much that I was willing to give it one last try. Because I had built a good relationship with my colleague, I felt comfortable pressing it on her a bit.

I was initially frustrated by her lack of action. To be honest, I took it personally. It turns out that she only really heard me the last time—and that one time was all she needed. The problem was that I didn't know that she hadn't heard me before. Had I not overcommunicated, the idea never would have been realized, and the organization and my First-in-Command would have missed out on some incredible accomplishments as a result. As such, Overcommunicate is Stage 5 of the 2iC Excellence Framework (Figure 13).

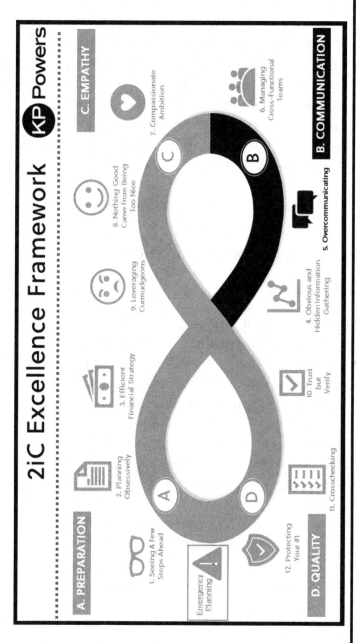

Figure 13 2iC Excellence Framework—Overcommunicate—Stage 5.

Overcommunicating: What It Means in Action

While it can be frustrating to repeat yourself in different ways, it's a lot like painting a room in your home. It's easy to see the first coat of paint, especially if it's a new color. However, a single coat can be uneven and splotchy. If you want the room to look right, you have to apply a second coat of paint. Comparing a wall with two coats to a wall with just one, it is clear that the second coat looks so much better. The extra repetitive effort paid off.

The Value of Overcommunicating

Message Received?

You took the time to craft a message and sent it via email or shared it in a meeting. It contained all of the details that recipients needed to know. Yet somehow, some people may have never got it (even though they received and read the email or were in the meeting). It can be very frustrating when people miss key points you're trying to make, but the fact is that the average person hears only 25% of the information communicated to them.

Saying or sending something once is not enough to ensure the message has been received.

The importance of overcommunicating can't be overstated. Organizations that communicate with their employees by sharing broadly and openly enjoy higher employee engagement and lower turnover rates.

> Your ability to coach the people around you is a huge part of your role as a Second-in-Command,

explains Sonali Kothari, Founder of Zolidar & Executive Coach, Kothari Leadership. This means effectively communicating—including overcommunicating—to ensure that the recipient received and understood the message.

Same Message, Different Words and Approach

As a Second-in-Command, it's your responsibility to support your First-in-Command by communicating and overcommunicating to the various teams in the organization what you are doing. Additionally, Firsts-in-Command count on their 2iCs to overcommunicate on their behalf. The value of repeating a message shared by the First-in-Command is significant.

A Harris Poll study of business leaders and knowledge workers estimates the cost of poor communication in the workplace at $12,506 per employee per year (Grammarly, 2022). While that may not seem like much money, it adds up quickly over the course of an employee's tenure at the organization. For businesses with 50 employees, that equates to more than $600,000; for those with 500 employees, the staggering price tag is more than $6 million (Grammarly, 2022).

Quality communication and overcommunication translate to company savings. Imagine the accomplishments that could be achieved by redirecting those funds to employee training and professional development, ergonomic furniture, product development, or returns to shareholders.

As Second-in-Command, you are a different yet familiar voice to many in the organization. As such, you can communicate the First-in-Command's message in a complementary way that resonates differently with people, expanding its reach. Some employees may feel more comfortable asking the 2iC questions, or they need time to digest the initial message and have a well-formed question when the 2iC brings up the topic.

Joseph Allen, higher education, customer service, and student success leader, says,

> Never underestimate the power of responsive communication, whether it is digitally, by phone, or in person.

Overcommunicating key messages to ensure that critical information gets through to the folks who need it the most is almost a requirement for a 2iC. A "one and done" approach simply isn't going to suffice.

Benefits of Overcommunicating

Higher rates of employee engagement lead to higher retention. This isn't a new insight. Over the last several decades, many studies have concluded as much. Seasoned leaders know that it's the case, and many employees have both positive and negative stories that serve as anecdotal evidence.

However, there is a new twist: It's getting harder for all organizations to retain employees. Programs and efforts that once led to high levels of retention have either become the norm or are not desirable to new generations or a remote workforce. For example, in-person employee engagement events are of no value to employees who work from home. Employers now have to offer benefits that set them apart from other organizations (Young Entrepreneur Council, 2022) while dealing with an elongated hiring process—18% longer than prior to the pandemic (Wiles, 2021).

As will be discussed in the section on compassionate ambition (Stage 7), overcommunicating can help with retention by filling in information gaps so that employees don't feel like they are missing out on something or being kept out of the loop. Providing those missing pieces can help people feel like they are not being excluded. For example, when a company decides to make significant changes to the organization structure (i.e., "a re-org"), it can be very stressful for impacted employees. Releasing information too soon results in questions that the leadership cannot answer or poorly thought-out plans. Waiting too long to share information leave employees to try to get tidbits from whomever they can so as to fill in the information gaps.

Filling in the Information Gaps

When people don't have all or most of the information they need, they begin to fill in the gaps on their own. The reality they imagine is almost always a worse story than the actual truth, leading to undue stress and anxiety, not to mention lower productivity. As a Second-in-Command, part of your role is to be that information gap filler.

As a result, employees within the organization will begin to trust you because they will see you as someone who provided important missing information that they were not getting from their traditional sources (e.g., supervisor, co-workers, intranet, staff meetings). Private conversations make it possible to build trust even faster. (I'll go into more detail on trust when we reach Stage 10, Trust but Verify).

Trust is necessary in every direction—especially with your First-in-Command. The Dean of the United States University College of Education, Rebecca Wardlow, explains it this way,

> Trust is essential. And because I trust you (as a
> First-in-Command), and I believe that you've got the
> right vision and goals, there are times that trust just
> has to happen because of confidentiality and inability to get the whole picture.

Gathering Information of Your Own

These private conversations also benefit you as a 2iC since the other person will likely share information with you that they wouldn't have otherwise due to lack of opportunity or a reluctance to speak publicly. As a result, you gain a new perspective on the current situation and maybe even problems that are beginning to brew. You can either synthesize this new, unanticipated hidden information or file it away for use at a later date. One never knows when information gathered months or years ago will become valuable for moving a project forward.

The Impact of Undercommunicating

Unfortunately, goodwill can go bad when overcommunicating does not occur. A painful example comes to mind. I once knew an organization whose profits were not as high as usual. However, due to a particular series of circumstances, the senior leadership was committed to finding money to have a fully funded merit pool to recognize everyone's hard work. In this organization, the timing of merit raises took place at the same time as employee evaluations. Of course, as in every organization, managers were encouraged to differentiate between employees so that everyone was not given the same perfect score of 5 out of 5. In this case, managers were required to provide substantive feedback that employees could use to make a greater contribution to the organization. The message of using employee evaluations as a tool to grow employee skill sets was hammered home that year.

The committed C-suite leaders made some tough decisions to find the merit funds, cutting back on supplies and services. They wanted to make the fully funded merit pool a surprise and kept it quiet. Given the profit loss, most employees were not anticipating a merit increase.

When the company-wide email came out announcing that all employees would be receiving a 3% merit raise, everyone was stunned. The managers were also angry. The announcement was made immediately after employee evaluations were due—the same employee evaluations where Human Resources had repeated the message that employees who had contributed more to the organization be recognized for their efforts with higher scores.

The message from the C-suite leadership was, "We are expecting managers to do the courageous work of delivering honest feedback to employees, even if it is difficult. Don't give everyone the same score." However, these leaders did the exact opposite with the merit pool. They gave everyone the same merit increase, regardless of their evaluation results. Employees who got a 4.5 on their evaluation received the same increase as those who got a 2.8.

This really damaged relationships between senior leaders and managers and sent employees a mixed message. Top performers were left wondering why they should work so hard if everyone was going to get the same merit raise. Had C-suite leaders communicated and overcommunicated what was going to happen before the announcement, they would have received the same feedback that they got after the announcement went out and it was too late to rescind it. The only thing left for the senior leaders to do was apologize.

Take Action—Progress Over Perfection

Questions for Reflection and Discussion

1. When do you find yourself overcommunicating? Does it help achieve the results you want?
2. How can overcommunication be used at key points in the project such that overcommunication is adding value rather than annoying?

3. What methods do you use for overcommunication? Repetition? Variety of venues? Variation of message? Which is more effective for each of your audiences/groups?
4. What has been your most useful communication technique? Why? Take note of when you are using it. Under what conditions? How can you use it more?

Stage 6

Managing Cross-Functional Teams

There were tough problems to solve in organizations before the pandemic, and now there are more of them, as well as new challenges that no one ever anticipated. As an ambitious leader, when you spot a tough problem, you can: (1) ignore it and hope it goes away or someone else deals with it or (2) tackle it head-on and achieve phenomenal results.

Of course, one person can't handle all the tough problems. You need to be selective. But how do you decide which problems to take on? As such, Managing Cross-Functional Teams is Stage 6 of the 2iC Excellence Framework (Figure 14).

Managing Cross-Functional Teams: What It Means in Action

Have you noticed "cross-functional team management skills" as a requirement in any recent job postings or asked about them in interviews? I certainly have. But what does the term

DOI: 10.4324/9781003382003-9

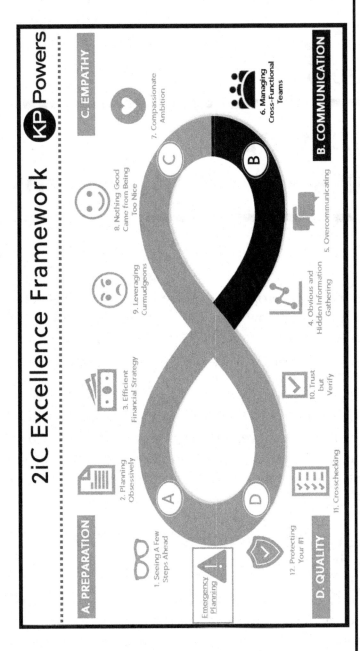

Figure 14 2iC Excellence Framework—Managing Cross-Functional Teams—Stage 6.

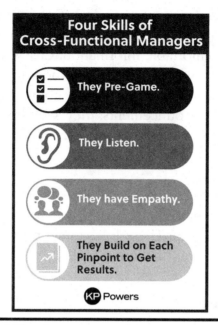

Figure 15   Four Skills of Cross-Functional Managers.

really mean? It sounds like a clever way of saying, "You'll need to manage a group of people who don't report to you."

There are always at least a few people with this special talent in any organization. They have an uncanny ability to read between the lines and build on common ground. That common ground may be a teeny-tiny pinpoint to stand on at first, but it's a start.

I'm intrigued by these people and observe them intently when I find them. I'd like to think that in my 20-plus years of improving organizations, I've picked up a few good tips from these folks—let's call them Cross-Functional Team Managers. Here are four skills that are worth developing if you want to be a better Cross-Functional Team Manager (Figure 15).

They Pre-Game

No, they aren't tailgating (though I'd bet they'd throw a heck of a tailgate). Instead, they meet with people to hear their comments and concerns on a topic *before* committee meet-ings. Since no one wants to be surprised in a meeting with negative or uncomfortable information, Cross-Functional Team Managers find out what they need to know in advance. They don't dictate what the meeting will be about, nor do they make "surprise'" announcements; they seek input and expertise to inform the meeting agenda and content.

They Listen

I mean really listen. They literally pause and think—in the middle of the meeting. These folks are comfortable sitting in silence to "digest" information in real-time.

They Have Empathy

Nearly 20 years ago, I read a sidebar in *Fortune* magazine indicating that empathy would be one of the most needed but also most lacking skills in the workplace over the next decade. Empathy? Nowadays technology keeps us connected to work 24/7, which leaves little downtime or opportunity for recharging. Good Cross-Functional Team Managers care about people and see each team member as a whole person. And they express that more often than just on someone's birthday.

They ask how employees are doing—both personally and professionally—and they pay attention to the answer. Also, they notice things—when a colleague wears a new shirt or if someone is consistently late to meetings. Good Cross-Functional Team Managers know who has been caring for an elderly parent or sick child; they make sure to check in on the well-being of both caregiver and patient. They know who is training for a marathon, and they ask them about their preparation. And they know who is working hard, going above and beyond, and would value professional recognition.

When they notice and acknowledge these things, they encourage the employees themselves *and* others on their cross-functional teams to be the best they can be.

They Build on Each Pinpoint to Get Results

After finding that pinpoint of common ground to stand on (as described above), they run with it. They get a team of people to move forward, building consensus with intention so that the pinpoint turns into a full landing pad. This often results in something new and exciting that could not have been accomplished without collaboration across multiple teams. "I'm a braider of ropes," says Joseph Allen, higher education, customer service, and student success leader. "I bring people (individual threads) together to make strong teams, processes, and institutional infrastructure."

The Value of Managing Cross-Functional Teams

Many people will shy away from managing a cross-functional team. It's harder to manage people who don't report to you than folks who do. Instead of motivating these individuals through annual employee evaluations, merit raises, and chain-of-command, you have to inspire them to participate and do their best work for some other reason. That's hard, but it gets easier with practice.

There's much to be gained from these interdisciplinary experiences, so Seconds-in-Command should seek out cross-functional team management opportunities rather than shying away from them. While I've noted the importance of relationships in earlier stages, one of the ways to learn *how* to build relationships—a key skill for 2iCs—is by leading cross-functional teams.

Stacey Gonzales, Ed.D., education leader, notes,

> As a Second-in-Command, my job is to identify the
> right people, get them in the room, figure out whose
> strengths are where, what the formation of the teams
> should be, and why we should have some cross-
> functional aspects or some not have cross-functional
> elements. I'm thinking through the dynamic of who's
> in that room in order to build those guiding coali-
> tions that set the entire team up for success.

Of course, part of the impetus to lead a cross-functional team
is to accomplish things that one team could not have done on
their own. But perhaps more important than completing
projects is the exclusive access you gain to new insights and
problems in the organization, as well as possible solutions
and capabilities, by participating in interdisciplinary teams.

The 2iC as a Cross-Functional Team Manager

When problems arise in an organization, they typically do not
affect a single department but rather multiple departments.
For this reason, not everyone has the combined skill set to
serve as a Cross-Functional Team Manager, and the demand
for those who do is high. Since Seconds-in-Command become
known for solving just about any problem—we simply dive in
and chip away at it until we figure it out—we often find
ourselves being tapped to lead cross-functional teams.

Some people will often find themselves feeling frustrated
because they are working with other team members who
don't report to them. Typically, a manager receives an auto-
matic level of authority simply because they are the supervisor
and in control of their subordinate's promotion and annual
review. Cross-functional team members are participating for
some other reason—maybe they enjoy the challenge of the
project, or they worked on a previous project with you, or you

asked their boss to put them on the team as a favor. It takes a lot more time, effort, and energy to motivate people when you're not their supervisor. However, in the long run, regardless of who reports to whom, motivation is a stronger strategy than leading by authority. While it's difficult to manage people that don't report to you, being able to do so is a hallmark skill for Seconds-in-Command to possess and continually develop.

Another advantage of serving as a Cross-Functional Team Manager is that it is noticed by leadership. Senior leaders can see that you know how to bring people together and get them focused on a common goal in an efficient, effective, and respectful way. Many Firsts-in-Command either don't have the time or haven't developed the skills to be a Cross-Functional Team Manager so they greatly value having a Second-in-Command that they can call on to serve in that role. "The culture amongst the Second-in-Command chain is so important. Having those individuals linked with you (the First-in-Command), signifying that we're all in this together and that everyone has each other's back, is critical," notes Education Consultant and Former Higher Education Executive Leader Jane McAuliffe, Ph.D.

> When people are in it for the wrong reasons or trying to stand out from the group, it just doesn't work. So, if you have everyone headed in the right direction, in it for the right reasons, you totally know you have each other's back, and you're supporting each other—then that link becomes so strong.

Benefits of Managing Cross-Functional Teams

The Problem No One Wants

Seconds-in-Command should look for the problems that no one else wants. If the problem exists and no one has successfully tackled it yet, people will be thrilled when you solve it. And because you are an ambitious leader, you are going to rock it! (You have only one speed—maximum success.) Since others likely have something to gain from solving the problem, it is also fairly easy to get folks in the organization to participate in a workgroup (more about managing cross-functional workgroups below).

You'll Likely Be the Only Cook in the Kitchen

If no one else wants to address the problem, you likely won't have competitors seeking to chair the workgroup. Leadership may even give you free rein to build a team to solve the problem, allowing you to select staff with the knowledge base and positive attitude required to work together effectively.

You'll Become a "Go-to" Person for the More Challenging Problems

When (not if) you succeed in taking on a tough problem and finding a solution, decision-makers will notice. And behind each set of tough problems visible to the masses is another layer of problems that only a subset of people knows about. Once you've demonstrated your problem-solving abilities, leadership may begin to seek your opinion and assistance with those other challenges.

You Can Build on Your Accomplishments

If you plan to stay at your current organization, tackling tough problems will keep you relevant. And if you are planning to leave (or aren't sure when you might), well, solving problems no one else has been able to address will help you assemble a list of significant accomplishments to share at future interviews. Perhaps this work could be a bridge to real professional growth!

There's a reason no one wants to deal with certain problems. But there are likely very good reasons why taking some of them on would be a terrific professional move for you. If you want to be noticed, sometimes you have to go where no one else has been willing to tread.

Take Action—Progress Over Perfection

Questions for Reflection and Discussion

1. Think about the Cross-Functional Team Managers you have at your organization. What tough problem did your Cross-Functional Team Managers solve that helped your organization achieve phenomenal results?
2. What is the next tough problem that a Cross-Functional Team Manager should tackle at your organization?
3. Does your organization have enough Cross-Functional Team Managers in your organization to achieve your ambitious goals?
4. Have you worked with any Cross-Functional Team Managers? What have you learned from them? What did they do that made the project and team members successful?

PHASE C

EMPATHY

Gone are the days when leaders focus only on profit. We know from research and analysis that organizations that care about their employees and their customers have healthier financials, more loyal customers, and greater satisfaction among employees and customers alike. While CEOs' and presidents' attention is still on the bottom line, 2iCs have an opportunity to elevate the organization's work through empathy and compassionate ambition. Phase C: Empathy, is the third of four phases in the 2iC Excellence Framework and includes three stages:

7. Compassionate Ambition
8. Nothing Good Came From Being Too Nice
9. Leverage Curmudgeons

DOI: 10.4324/9781003382003-10

Stage 7

Compassionate Ambition

The word *ambitious* has gotten a bad reputation. When someone is called "ambitious" it can be seen as a negative. As if achievements are a bad thing.

Rather, once someone is considered "too ambitious," the underlying message often is that the person is single-mindedly focused on achievements at the cost of other things (e.g., family, being kind, self-care, etc.). Just because someone is ambitious does not mean that they must be a jerk while chasing their goals. Quite the opposite.

About 15 years ago, I remember reading an article in a popular business magazine that empathy would be the next skill set senior leaders needed to develop. Indeed, empathy and its cousin—compassion—have finally become more part of today's workplace. Yet, there is still much work to do with infusing empathy and compassion into company culture, especially as it relates to ambition.

Seconds-in-Command are ambitious people who have mastered getting a lot of things done efficiently and effectively. They also tend to be very caring people, wanting to

DOI: 10.4324/9781003382003-11

help others—especially their First-in-Command. As such 2iCs naturally combine their caring and ambition strengths into Compassionate Ambition. As such, Compassionate Ambition is Stage 7 of the 2iC Excellence Framework (Figure 16).

Compassionate Ambition: What It Means in Action

What exactly is Compassionate Ambition? Compassionate Ambition contains three essential elements: enhancing strengths, distracting disadvantages, and motivating momentum (Figure 17).

Enhancing Strengths

Enhancing strengths allows leaders and team members to feel greater confidence in work that they are naturally, efficiently, and effectively good at. We all have talents. Everyone isn't good at the things we are good at—and vice versa. For example, some people (myself included) love planning, while others don't like to plan. The non-planners of the world are usually thrilled that the planners want to do the parts of a project that they don't like. Finding complementary strengths can be a huge advantage in team building. Amplifying each team member's strengths allows them to increase that strength even more by exercising it.

Start with each team member's strengths. What activities do you and your team naturally gravitate toward? Which does your group do well? What things do you focus on when you are asked what you do? Hint: People like to talk about the stuff they like to do generally. No one ever talks about their upcoming dentist appointment (unless for some reason they love going to the dentist).

Figure 16   2iC Excellence Framework—Compassionate Ambition—Stage 7.

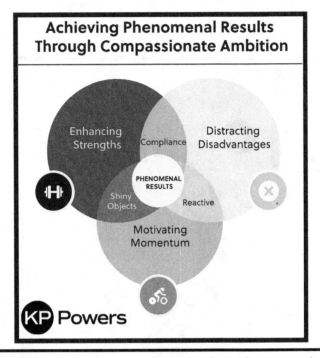

Figure 17   Achieving Phenomenal Results Through Compassionate Ambition.

Distracting Disadvantages

Yes, we all have them (weaknesses) or what I call distracting disadvantages. They are worse than weaknesses because we are lured into thinking that we can become experts with just a bit of effort. We get distracted, spending lots of time working to move something from a disadvantage to a strength. That doesn't mean our organizations can't be good at these things; it just isn't our natural calling. Take a company that achieves phenomenal results in tech and then begins to dabble in an adjacent offering. The ramp-up and expertise needed for the company to be as successful as it is with tech products is simply a mountain to climb—attainable, but is it worth it?

Distracting disadvantages take a ton of time for little gain. Think of a time when you dove into a new topic, issue, or hobby—one you didn't know anything about. Zilch. Did it take a while to identify trusted sources? Were you sorting through tons of information, including contradictory opinions? Did you invest a fair amount of time only to realize that you'd just scratched the surface? These are the distracting disadvantages—activities or subjects that you know little to nothing about and can't pick up without devoting a considerable amount of time (i.e., time suck).

For example, when you have a significant electrical or plumbing issue, you could (1) watch a bunch of YouTube videos, read a lot about it, learn from others that have done the work, (2) call a professional who can do it much faster, likely more safely, and possibly more cheaply because they have all the right tools, or (3) move. (Okay, moving is extreme, but it is an option.) If you haven't already mastered a topic or skill, put it in the distracting disadvantage category. That doesn't mean that you can't be great at it (someday), just that it will distract you from your existing strengths.

Some topics/skills are clearly beyond your capacities—heart surgery, for example. Others are just enough within reach than you might think, "I could give that a try." And there are plenty of television shows and YouTube channels encouraging us to give all kinds of things a go. Has anyone ever been inspired to tackle a home improvement project after watching one of HGTV's renovation shows and wound up with something that didn't look anything like it did on TV? A wasted weekend and a few hundred dollars later, we all realize that it might have been better to take a different approach. The goal is to save you from yourself by identifying those distracting disadvantages before they take away too much time from your true focus and prevent you from achieving phenomenal results. Stretching a little is good and can really complement your efforts. Stretching too much can cause an injury.

Motivating Momentum

Motivating momentum is the key ingredient. Most people can list their and their organization's strengths and disadvantages. For example, a tech company might say, "We are in the technology field. We definitely are not in the health service field." But what does one *do* with this information? Great—we know our strengths and disadvantages. Now what? Well, what motivates you? What would get you up and going? What would give your team momentum?

In this post-pandemic world, businesses and organizations no longer have access to a plentiful labor market. While some economists believe that a recession will correct the labor market woes, forward-thinkers have noted that the labor shortage was inevitable before the pandemic. The pandemic just made it much worse. And the labor shortage isn't going away now that the pandemic has subsided.

Leaders and managers within businesses and organizations have a tall task in front of them: to achieve phenomenal results with a smaller and/or limited team. This makes identifying the motivating momentum more critical than ever before. Many ambitious leaders can identify the strengths and distracting disadvantages of their team members and organizations (e.g., SWOT analyses). However, digging in to get to know team members, co-workers, and the organization well enough to identify their motivating momentum is the modern-day ambitious leader differentiator.

What is exciting to each of your team members? What would really motivate your team or organization to make progress on a game-changing task? This generally requires thinking more deeply about the people involved and what they really care about. For example, I recently worked with an organization that couldn't get motivated about some compliance tasks (shocking!). After learning more about the CEO and what motivated him and guiding him, the CEO became a champion of the effort and began developing a new set of standards that exceeded those required for compliance. No longer was the company focused on compliance; they were motivated by a desire to be *the best*. That shift created the momentum to achieve phenomenal results.

Compassionate Ambition in the Overlaps

Now let's go another layer deeper to explore how these three components (enhancing strengths, distracting disadvantages, and motivating momentum) overlap.

Compliance

When enhancing strengths and distracting disadvantages overlap, teams or organizations often focus on minimum standards. What do we need to do to pass? What are the minimum criteria to be found in compliance?

Shiny Objects

The shiny object is quite alluring. It comes at the right time and the right place. You see someone else and their organization (with lesser skills and resources) successfully achieving results and you think, "I've got more skills, expertise, and resources than so-and-so." You are motivated by possibilities and fall victim to shiny-object syndrome. This is largely because distracting disadvantages and their complementary elements weren't considered.

Reactive

We all have things we don't want to do (attend a meeting that should be an email, fill out that form, have difficult conversations, etc.). Eventually, however, we need to do the work. While the distracting disadvantages aren't our strength or natural attraction, motivating momentum pushes us to be reactive. For example, if doing annual evaluations isn't your favorite task, deadlines from Human Resources to complete them will provide some momentum to get things done, putting you, your team, and/or your organization into a reactive mode.

The Value and Benefits of Compassionate Ambition

Leading by Executive Order

A more outdated leadership style commonly used was to issue edicts rather than explaining the "why" behind what they were doing. Three to four decades of analysis of leadership styles and their relationship to company growth and profits as well as employee satisfaction and retention revealed that there is a better way.

We've learned that the dictator model does not yield long-term benefits and that its short-term benefits are minimal at best. It's simply not a positive work environment. Further, younger generations are not only uninterested in working in a dictator model, but they also reject it unapologetically by calling it out on social media. Many leaders have come to see the error of their ways as new leadership patterns and habits emerged in the form of thought leadership as well as trainings and workshops.

Employee-Centered Management

In the studies, a common trait emerged among successful organizations: a focus on employees. Managers who showed compassion for their employees built stronger relationships and trust with them. In turn, loyalty to the manager and a compassionate company culture resulted and thus lower turnover rates and higher profits.

A Second-in-Command has a responsibility that's bigger than themselves; the responsibility to be

inclusive, develop others, and assist others in building relationships,

explains Jacquie Furtado, Director of Strategy & Outcomes at
San Diego State University's Academy for Professional
Excellence.

Of course, there will always be some people who reject
any leadership style. The skeptics that reject compassionate
leadership tend to see compassion as a weakness rather than
a strength. In their view, being compassionate means not
being ambitious.

I would argue that compassion actually serves a Second-in-
Command's ambition. Compassionate ambition is a tactic that
2iCs can adopt as part of their strategic toolset. They can still
push ahead and still move the needle to achieve the company's goals while being empathetic. Higher levels of engagement, lower turnover rates, and higher quality products or
services are among the benefits to employers of creating and
maintaining a compassionate workplace.

Compassionate ambition is about meeting people where
they are as humans, gaining an understanding of what drives
them, and then showing them that you, as a leader, whether
you're the Second-in-Command or the manager of a team, are
there to support the team and the project. Ultimately, people
want to do a good job and want to have accomplishments, and
if they have a compassionate leader helping them, they will be
that much more inspired to get their job done and do it well.

Take Action—Progress Over Perfection

Questions for Reflection and Discussion

1. Who do you think of as an example of someone having
   empathy and compassion while they are being ambitious?

Someone within your organization? A national or famous person? What is it about their actions that stand out to you?

2. How can you be ambitious and a positive force for your company?

3. What do you think are the most important attributes, skills, and abilities to be a leader with compassionate ambition?

4. What traits do you currently have that contribute to your compassionate ambition? What are some times where those skills served you well?

5. What traits do you want to develop to enhance your compassionate ambition skill set?

Stage 8

Nothing Good Came From Being Too Nice

Imagine (Figure 18) a scale from left to right, with the left being "availability" and the right being "advantage." The center, where one is available without being taken advantage of, is ideal. Seconds-in-Command often find themselves being too available and quickly slip over to the "advantage" side of the scale through no one's fault or ill intentions.

Seconds-in-Command often tell me how much they enjoy their First-in-Command and ultimately their organization. The topic of making themselves available to their First-in-Command came up in many interviews for this book. Several interviewees that have served as a 2iC commented that they were often perceived as being too nice (as if being very kind were a weakness or a fault).

The words are different for each person, but the theme and stages all follow a similar pattern: At first, the 2iC offers to help on a topic outside their current scope of work. Because 2iCs are well known for figuring things out, folks accept the assistance.

DOI: 10.4324/9781003382003-12

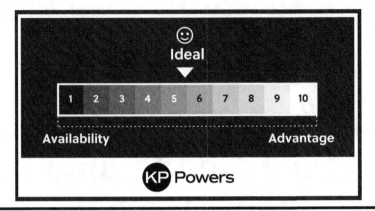

Figure 18 Availability to Advantage Scale.

The Nice Trap

The situation is supposed to be temporary (e.g., serving in an interim role, or working on a special project). However, because Seconds- in-Command are overachievers, their deliverables for the project impress people. As a result, the temporary becomes semi-permanent as the 2iC is asked to work on the project when it occurs again (e.g., annual report) or for an extended period of time (e.g., delaying hiring a permanent employee).

The 2iC accepts because they did offer to help, after all. The First-in-Command views the ask as acceptable because the 2iC offered and seems to enjoy the work, as evidenced by their phenomenal accomplishments without complaint. The First-in-Command might even push the ask to expand the scope of work.

This pattern repeats itself multiple times until the 2iC realizes they are no longer on the availability side of the scale, finding joy in helping. Instead, the Second-in-Command has landed on the "advantage" side of the scale. It happened so slowly that they can't pinpoint when they tipped over the line, but they know they are now squarely on the right-hand side.

Unfortunately, 2iCs have created precedents for such circumstances and advertised their availability. Exacerbating the problem, Firsts-in-Command are taking Seconds-in-Command at their word when they say they want to be involved and are willing to dive in. There is also a bit of an intrapersonal conflict for 2iCs as they do generally want to be available.

Just like anyone else, though, 2iCs have their breaking point. They have a difficult time shedding their reputation for being available all the time for any need, day or night, but while the scope creep to being taken advantage of is slow, the trip back to the availability zone is not so gradual. It can be quite abrupt.

In fact, many people are caught off-guard when 2iCs find that they have spread themselves too thin and can't continue in the same way anymore. Some 2iCs shared that these events led to their resignation. Others found new and better solutions—for everyone—within their organizations. As such, Nothing Good Came From Being Too Nice is Stage 8 of the 2iC Excellence Framework (Figure 19).

Nothing Good Came From Being Too Nice: What It Means in Action

As 2iCs, we often look like we are successfully and happily spinning plates while juggling. The truth is, 2iCs do enjoy having multiple and different projects to work on. We thrive on solving puzzles. And yes, we love to help others.

So what's wrong with that? Aren't these desirable characteristics in an employee? There's nothing wrong with having these characteristics. Employers, and especially Firsts-in-Command, really want, need, and value these 2iC traits. What they don't want is a surprise resignation. A First-in-Command counts on the 2iC for a lot of important things, including managing their own availability. It is up to you to say when

Figure 19 2iC Excellence Framework—Nothing Good Came From Being Too Nice—Stage 8.

there is a problem and identify possible alternatives and solutions long before you consider drafting your resignation letter.

While we 2iCs think that we are being helpful or nice and never take the time to reflect on our workload before it gets unmanageable, the truth is that too much "nice" often catches up with us, too much "nice" can lead to not-so-nice consequences.

Turning the Narrative

When working with 2iCs, I often ask them, "What would you do if you saw too many things on your First-in-Command's plate?" and "What would you do if you saw the 1iC making decisions such that would take everyone down a chaotic road?"

Without fail, they rattle out their response like they would their phone number, something they know without having to think about it. They say something to the effect of: "I would bring my observations to my 1iC's attention, presenting the information, my care and concern, along with potential solutions. I would emphasize that their actions impact all of us, so it is important that they hear what I have to say."

This next part can hurt a bit, but I then ask the 2iC, "Have you ever considered applying those strategies to your 2iC role?" Very quickly, they begin connecting the dots. While it can feel great to help and be nice, the phrase (and title of the Stage) "Nothing good ever came from being nice" is a powerful reminder that niceness without boundaries and regular self-evaluation isn't a good long-term strategy.

The Value of the Concept That Nothing Good Came From Being Too Nice

One of the benefits of applying this concept as a Second-in-Command is to remind yourself that being kind is not the same as being nice. More kindness is needed in this world.

However, being nice is not the same as being kind. Furthermore, being nice is an indicator for some that you can be taken advantage of or pushed and stretched more than others without being offended or saying no.

This is particularly important for Seconds-in-Command because many are "helpers" and often find themselves with heavy workloads because their curious minds say yes to every opportunity. Additionally, because 2iCs are really good at figuring out tangly projects, we get a lot of those thrown our way. The problem is that because we do such a great job on projects, folks are perfectly fine with handing them over to us for good. As a result, the scope of work gets larger and larger.

Remember, these workload increases all came from being "nice."

Benefits of Nothing Good Came From Being Too Nice

Like compassion (Stage 7: Compassionate Ambition), being nice can and does have its misperceptions. As a Second-in-Command, having a reputation for being nice can impede your ability to access information or move forward on some projects.

Indeed, one of the challenges that Seconds-in-Command often have is being too nice. Being too nice is a double-edged sword because while you want to be seen as approachable, that desire can quickly take you into the category of "too nice," which leads to a slippery slope of getting taken advantage of. However, you need to be approachable to gather information and get tasks done for your First-in-Command. As a result, you end up struggling to appear just friendly and welcoming enough that others will be willing to share information with you—but not too nice.

The Advantage of Pushing Back

Seconds-in-Command can surprise their co-workers when they push back or enforce consequences for bad behavior. For example, when a 2iC is perceived as being too nice, others in the organization might start abusing that niceness through uncooperative behavior such as not meeting deadlines, canceling meetings at the last minute, or working against the 2iC's explicit goals and strategies.

While everyone has a bad day, and we all would like a little grace for mistakes, when a regular pattern of disrespect and cavalier attitude emerges, the issue must be addressed. This is when the surprise happens. The offender never expects the 2iC, who is so nice, to object to their actions. When called out for their bad behavior, the employee generally knows that they were being disrespectful. Would they have said those things to their supervisor or canceled meetings with another senior leader? Even so, it is difficult for the employee to admit that they were wrong.

Some sternness and resetting of appropriate behaviors and boundaries can communicate to others that maybe you aren't so nice after all. When I've found myself in these situations and I reflect on my role in the reputation of niceness, I can usually identify a project or event where I was too nice, cracking open the door for advantage-taking to begin.

As a result, I'm still nice, but I am mindful about being too nice.

While it is important to remember the phrase "Nothing ever good came from being too nice," a lot of good can come from being approachable, collegial, and cooperative. You don't have to be a jerk to get things done; there are professional, tactical ways to move things forward productively. However, as a Second-in-Command responsible for managing up, down, and sideways, it's especially important to remember that you're better off being approachable than nice.

Take Action—Progress Over Perfection

Questions for Reflection and Discussion

1. What's the difference between a 2iC that is helpful, yet still an independent thinker and one who is too helpful?
2. What do you think the biggest things are that a First-in-Command looks for in a 2iC?
3. How do you balance being too nice with gathering information and getting tasks done as a Second-in-Command?
4. How do you strike a balance between being approachable and getting things done for your First-in-Command?
5. How do you balance being approachable and still appear assertive?
6. Who have you worked with (current or former organizations) that is able to not be too nice while still accomplishing goals? What are one to two things that they did? Can you utilize some of their strategies?

Stage 9

Leveraging Curmudgeons

Every organization has at least one curmudgeon; most have a few. I have a theory that every organization must have more than one because it seems more than a coincidence that multiple curmudgeons—across multiple organizations—work together through a sophisticated network to wreak havoc on productive people from time to time. How else do we explain the coincidence that overachievers at multiple organizations experience chaos orchestrated by curmudgeons in the same week? A colleague (Simmie A. Raiford) and I noticed this phenomenon a few decades ago as we would call each other for support and venting. We began to notice that these events took place on Wednesdays.

Jack-Ass Wednesday

We began to refer to these curmudgeon-initiated events as JAW—Jack-Ass Wednesday. When the week is especially hectic, the W stands for week. While JAW references a single day, Wednesday, we came to realize that the event lasted more

DOI: 10.4324/9781003382003-13

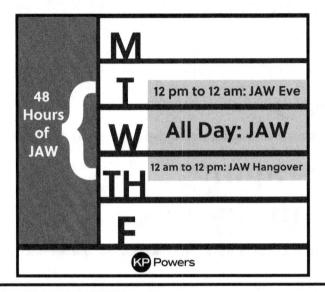

Figure 20   48 Hours of JAW.

than 24 hours. In fact, JAW spanned a full 48 hours. Jack-Ass Eve begins at 12 noon on Tuesday and continues through Jack-Ass Hangover, at 12 noon on Thursday (Figure 20).

Our theory is that Wednesday is when people are furthest from the weekend in any direction. This makes them extra cranky, and they take it out on those around them.

Many 2iCs have shared that while managing Cross-Functional Teams (Stage 6) they often encounter someone who makes the project 10 times harder, throwing boulders in the project's path and making it more difficult, but not impossible, to succeed.

The curmudgeons tend to make just enough valid points that leadership listens to them. It turns out the curmudgeons aren't wrong; it is the way they deliver information that needs a lot of coaching.

2iCs have a choice: Either ignore the curmudgeons completely, knowing that they have access to leaders who will listen to them, or figure out how best to bring them and their crass comments under the tent and use their information to your advantage. As such, Leverage Curmudgeons is Stage 9 of the 2iC Excellence Framework (Figure 21).

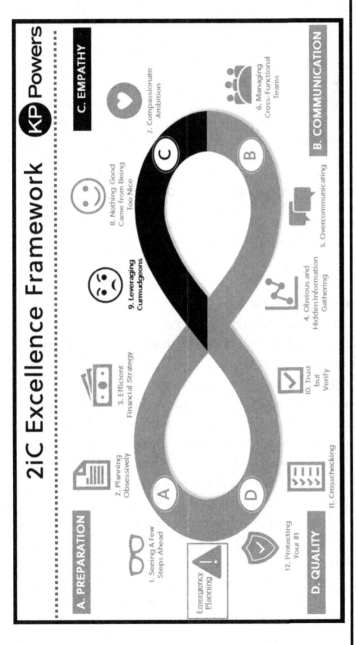

Figure 21 2iC Excellence Framework—Leverage Curmudgeons—Stage 9.

Leveraging Curmudgeons: What It Means in Action

Since curmudgeons exist and aren't going away anytime soon, it's important for 2iCs to figure out how to keep them from slowing progress. To be clear, you should consider it a win if you can move a curmudgeon from putting boulders in the way to using speedbumps. It is unrealistic to think that curmudgeons will opt for a smooth, unobstructed road.

What Curmudgeons Have in Common

Having dealt with my fair share of curmudgeons and heard other 2iCs' curmudgeon stories, I have found a few common threads:

1. Curmudgeons think they are doing a good day's work. They aren't actually trying to make your life harder. There is an easy test for this: If the curmudgeon throws up obstacles for others at the organization, it's not about you. Curmudgeons see it as a sense of duty to point out problems and advocate hard for a particular outcome.
2. Curmudgeons are a winning combination of right-enough and loud. Often others don't oppose them for one of two reasons: (1) they don't want to battle the curmudgeon publicly or (2) they don't know or care enough about the topic to stand toe to toe.
3. Curmudgeons have some good points, but these are overshadowed by their delivery. Curmudgeons are so annoying in how they present the information (shouting, wrong place, wrong time) that it is not well received. Truth be told, though, they aren't wrong (*Ugh!*).

Bringing the Curmudgeon Into the Fold

This last point—that the curmudgeons aren't wrong—is the hardest part to admit because we don't want to give them positive reinforcement and encourage them to continue their unpleasant behavior. For this reason, curmudgeons need to be engaged early in the process and privately. This makes curmudgeons feel like they have an opportunity to influence the project from the outset and gives 2iCs the advantage of incorporating the curmudgeon's information in a way that can benefit the project rather than hinder it.

Attribution to the curmudgeon is key. This may seem counterintuitive, but since the curmudgeon has a well-established barrier, most people will not go against the curmudgeon. If others learn that the curmudgeon has been involved in the project's development, it can be perceived that the curmudgeon has given their endorsement and that others who follow the curmudgeon's lead should also give their endorsement.

After a few projects or iterations like this, the curmudgeon will begin to seek out the 2iC to share thoughts and ideas. And since the curmudgeon has a well-established history of not being wrong, the curmudgeon, utilized correctly, can be a project accelerator. The curmudgeon begins to see the 2iC as an ally and translator, able to say the things they struggle to communicate.

In short, don't avoid curmudgeons; meet them head-on with a purposeful strategy. If you are constantly circumventing them, you will exhaust yourself and not accomplish as much work. 2iCs have to be willing to befriend folks they don't like (to a point). If you can roll away the boulders blocking the road, there will be fewer detours for the entire team.

The Value of Leveraging Curmudgeons

Curmudgeons waste precious resources such as time, energy, joy, and money. They really take the positivity out of projects and simply make things a lot harder than they need to be. Every organization has curmudgeons—they're everywhere. There is no way to eradicate curmudgeons from the workplace. We *have* to deal with them by finding a constructive way to bring them under the tent.

Because they're so incredibly difficult to deal with, curmudgeons can be a big reason why people leave an organization. They know how to cause a ruckus without getting fired. Part of your role as a Second-in-Command is to embrace these curmudgeons and really determine how to draw them into the fold and channel their very unique skill sets for good rather than bad.

One upside is that curmudgeons do not operate in secrecy. Most organizations already know who their curmudgeons are. Every organization has them, and as you're reading this, you've probably already thought of two or three you've encountered on the job.

The Negative Energy of Curmudgeons

The downside of curmudgeons is that they can sap the energy from a meeting or a process or an email thread, bringing other folks down in a very counterproductive way. Even if they aren't deliberately throwing up a roadblock or actively avoiding doing their share of the work, the negativity that they bring into a project is sure to deflate the group's efforts.

By frequently protesting others' suggestions and good ideas, a single curmudgeon can counter the collective positive energy of the group. Curmudgeons are empowered by someone; otherwise, they would be terminated. However, because they have longevity in the organization and deep knowledge of important matters (e.g., the only person who knows how to run payroll for the entire organization), they almost hold the organization hostage by causing enough problems to be counterproductive but not enough to get fired; the organization needs their knowledge, which they refuse to share with others.

Curmudgeons also feel empowered by their informal curmudgeon role as they know that they will not be terminated. They can't be let go because they know the most about essential systems. If they were fired, it would take three or four people full-time to replace that knowledge. They know this and use it to their advantage to bring negativity and pessimism into an otherwise energetic and ambitious workplace.

Benefits of Leveraging Curmudgeons

From the Second-in-Command perspective, one of the hardest things is preventing them from getting in your way. You must learn how to work around and/or with them or even befriend them. One strategy is to do something for the curmudgeon that makes them realize your value to them so that they will want to help you in the future. This can include getting information or a deliverable to the curmudgeon ahead of schedule or supporting their point in a meeting (assuming it's something you would have supported anyway).

Taking Control of the Curmudgeon Narrative

Since the curmudgeons will make their voices and opinion heard, the next thing to do is arrange the forum—literally plan for it. Giving the curmudgeon the microphone can take the form of a one-on-one meeting early in the project or scheduling them for the group agenda. Your goal as a 2iC is to get the curmudgeon to share their real issues sooner rather than later so that you can address them. The curmudgeon's goal is to be heard, recognized, and valued for their thinking.

It is the job of the Second-in-Command to unravel the unspoken issues that the curmudgeon is trying to raise. This requires the 2iC to peer into the cracks and crevices of what motivates the curmudgeon and what they care about so as to garner their support to move the entire group and project forward. Trying to combat the curmudgeon with logic is typically unproductive (although it can work for some more data-oriented minds).

Take Action—Progress Over Perfection

Questions for Reflection and Discussion

1. How do you effectively manage curmudgeons? What are some effective methods that you see from others when managing curmudgeons?
2. What are some early indicators that someone may be a curmudgeon? What actions do you take to leverage the curmudgeon for good?
3. Can you think of a time when a curmudgeon added value to a project? How did the leader get the curmudgeon to be a positive participant rather than a detractor? Could those tactics be used with other curmudgeons?
4. What are you doing today to build a relationship with the curmudgeons you know you will need to work with?

PHASE D

QUALITY

We all want value for the things we purchase. Quality becomes even more important for organizations driven by external evaluators such as compliance regulators, accreditors, and shareholders. This final section focuses on the key differentiator of quality. Seconds-in-Command are in a position to take quality to new levels that will give the organization a competitive advantage. Phase D: Quality is the last of the four phases in the 2iC Excellence Framework and includes three stages:

10. Trust but Verify
11. Crosschecking
12. Protecting Your #1

DOI: 10.4324/9781003382003-14

Stage 10

Trust but Verify

As heavily compliance-driven and regulated as the healthcare industry is, mistakes are still made. Recently, a colleague of mine was given a checkout form for the next steps. She was told she needed more tests. For a few weeks, my already very worry-prone colleague consulted Dr. Google and thought she had every ailment that ever existed. Her brother came to visit her. She, of course, couldn't resist talking about it with him and getting his opinion.

My colleague and the medical staff had made a major mistake—huge! Her brother noticed it right away: "Why isn't your name at the top of the page? It looks like this document is for someone else." My colleague had pored over this form many times and missed the first thing at the top of the page— the patient's name.

As a 2iC, you trust that the data and information you receive from your co-workers, employees, and leaders is accurate. They are part of your team, after all. However, there are times when even trustworthy sources may not provide accurate data. This can happen for any number of reasons— from human error to bias or simply because the information obtained is outdated and no longer relevant. It's important to

DOI: 10.4324/9781003382003-15

remember to trust, but verify so that you don't make decisions based on unverified information.

I've found that many people really don't know how to verify the information they are being provided. They will simply trust it is correct and move on. I've also found that this can lead to disappointment as well as a waste of time, having made a decision from wrong or outdated information.

Since quality information is critical to a 2iC's success, Trust but Verify is Stage 10 of the 2iC Excellence Framework (Figure 22).

Trust but Verify: What It Means in Action

Organizations that are subject to compliance and regulations have been using the trust but verify concept for decades. For example, in health care, patients are asked their name and date of birth each time they move from room to room or medical staff member to medical staff member. Why? Because the medical personnel are trusting that the paperwork outside the door belongs to the person inside. To verify, they simply ask the patient to confirm their name and date of birth.

Not only is it still important to trust but verify in compliance and regulated industries, doing so should be standard practice even when laws don't require it. 2iCs in all industries regularly use trust but verify. This one simple yet highly effective tool can significantly improve quality as well as the customer experience.

A Case in Point—The Problem

I'll share an example from my early days as a 2iC. My first job out of college was as an admissions advisor for my alma mater, SUNY Brockport (outside of Rochester, New York). The head of the transfer team was training me on how to review

Figure 22   2iC Excellence Framework—Trust But Verify—Stage 10.

applications for freshman admissions. He was a more senior person in the office. While he headed up transfer admissions, he knew a lot about freshman admissions too. Sometimes a person will apply as a transfer student because they have some credits, but they are really a freshman applicant. For this reason, he needed a solid command of the freshman application process to do transfer admissions.

Since he was passionate about transfer admissions, he regularly shared tangential information about related policies and procedures. He was thorough in his training, trying to give me the full picture, even though I didn't see some of the details. As an avid learner, I soaked it up.

He went through each field of the paper application, explaining each element. (Yes, this was back in the days of paper applications.) We got to the question: "Are you a transfer student?" The options were Yes or No. He paused, sighed, and emphatically said, "This is one of the most important questions on this application. Sometimes the applications can get misfiled as a freshman application even though the application is clearly marked as 'transfer' on this question." This key question was buried in the application.

This is where he showed his irritation with the process. "So, if the application is put in the freshman review drawers and the freshman review team—which you are part of— reviews the file and you miss this question, it causes all kinds of problems. Since they are a transfer student, their review process is more complex, and they need to have their transfer credits evaluated. If that transfer review never happens because their application is sitting in the freshman files, the student is left waiting for a decision letter because their file isn't completed. We can't have our students waiting unnecessarily."

Clearly frustrated by this issue, he reiterated, "This is an important question, and you need to get this right!" I wrote down in my notes that the transfer question was very important and circled it. I didn't need to write that down, though. His level of discomfort around the issue told me all I needed to know.

A Case in Point—My Solution

With my application review training complete and the first set of paper files in front of me, I began my review, paying extremely close attention to the transfer question. After I'd gone through about a dozen files, I began to question myself: "Did I check the transfer question on that last one?" Ugh—I had to go back and check. After doing that a few times, I realized that I needed a better system. I detest reworking—what a waste of time!

I decided to make a little check mark next to the transfer question response, which forced me to look at the response on every application. That way, I could be confident that I had looked at the response—and prove it! This was my way of trusting that the file was properly filed in the freshman review drawers but verifying that it was not in fact a transfer application. The process worked. I caught applications that needed to be rerouted to the transfer team. I felt good that I was sparing students an unnecessary wait by routing their applications correctly.

Fast-forward about a month later, and the head of transfer admissions came to my office. With his high energy, he always seemed to appear quickly out of nowhere. He asked, "Are you the one who made this check mark next to the transfer-in question?" I couldn't tell if I was in trouble or if he had had an extra dose of caffeine that day. I said, "Yes, I did." He asked why, and I explained, "You said that was the most important question on the application because it determined which review process the student received, which could slow down the decision if the student was routed through the wrong process."

He nodded his head as if he was proud that he had trained me and that I had retained the information he had taught me. I said, "Well, I found myself double-checking the transfer question, having to go back a few times. I began putting a check mark so I would know whether or not I had reviewed the question. It helps me to verify that the student is really a freshman applicant rather than a transfer. That mark is just for me so that I know for my own sanity that I checked the response."

He said, "That's brilliant. I have been telling other advisors for years that they need to review that question more thoroughly. I couldn't get people to change their process. I'm going to make this a new rule for my entire team." And as quickly as he had appeared in the doorway of my office, he was gone.

I'd thought he was going to cry. He was so passionate about transfer students, and someone had finally heard what he was really saying and addressed it with a solution that he could share. Trust but verify had a huge impact on him and on tens of thousands of future transfer students.

In short, it's worth taking the time to verify the information because doing so could result in significant savings. People make mistakes and can leave out or overlook details.

The Value of Trust but Verify

As noted earlier, people for the most part come to work every day wanting to do the very best that they can. But the truth is that people are people, and they will make mistakes.

Everyone makes mistakes. We're human, and even in the most heavily regulated industries and thorough processes, there will be errors. Since perfection isn't possible, 2iCs are instead trying to catch as many mistakes as they can.

Six Sigma

For example, Six Sigma is a suite of techniques and concepts focusing on increasing quality. The Six Sigma framework enables managers to determine if mistakes exceed acceptable—but very high—thresholds. So that all employees can have a common knowledge base in Six Sigma, the framework is structured in levels called "belts," each of which is a different color—white, yellow, green, black, and master black.

One of the most valuable lessons learned in my Six Sigma Black Belt training was that perfection isn't possible. Six Sigma advocates striving instead for near perfection—or six standard deviations.

Most pictures of a normal distribution curve show three standard deviations. With 99.7% of instances or cases falling within three standard deviations, there typically is little need to discuss any more than that. However, with six standard deviations, Six Sigma takes quality up three additional deviations, getting as close to 100% as possible—and even six deviations are considered a reach and quite exemplary. Even at the Six Sigma level, though, mistakes are still expected and permissible.

Perfection Isn't Possible, but Verifying Helps

Even though we know perfection isn't an option, 2iCs leverage the trust-but-verify concept to ensure the highest quality possible. Verifying the quality of a deliverable that has already been worked on by experts adds another layer of review.

Everything needs to be checked to some extent. Checks and balances are required to account for human error because it will happen. And if you don't do the necessary checking, then you're the one who just made the error. You need to be continually verifying work that people are doing, especially as a Second-in-Command. You owe it to your First-in-Command to be doing the verification work because they probably don't have the time or even the necessary awareness of the details to perform the level of review that a 2iC can.

The First-in-Command is trusting you to verify the work of others on their behalf. While no one expects perfection, there is an expectation of intentional effort to improve quality by setting up systematic ways to catch errors. Each issue you question or error you spot draws additional value from the entire team because it causes them to take another look at the deliverable.

A Fresh Perspective Through Verification

There have been numerous times when I have asked a question about a data file that has prompted the developer to look at the code again, only to find a different issue than the one I raised. I probably would never have asked about the issue that they found. However, it was my question that prompted the developer to look at the code with a fresh set of eyes.

Verification is an obligation of every leader, especially the Second-in-Command, as is building an understanding of that into the management culture. You need to make sure that other folks embody a philosophy of quality control because if one team is not taking the time to do quality checks or verification, it could have detrimental effects on other teams by perpetuating inferior work.

Verification is not the responsibility of one person. Seconds-in-Command should look to install systems of verification that complement their own reviews. Systems that enable verifications and are part of the culture are ideal. If you're not finding errors, then something is actually wrong with the process because no one can be perfect. I'll reread a document or an email multiple times because I know I'm not perfect. I know that there's a mistake somewhere. Sometimes I'll play a game with myself: "There must be an error, so where is it? How quickly can I find it?"

Benefits of Trust but Verify

When Verification Is Skipped, More Mistakes Occur

An organization once asked me to review a data file that had been submitted for a legal request. The opposing side said the file was incomplete and missing customers. The client didn't believe that the opposing side could know more about their data than they did. How did they know customers were missing? Were they just hedging? The client felt certain that their data file was accurate because they had submitted other files in previous years without any issues.

It turned out that the opposing side knew customers were missing from the file because their complainant was missing from the list. Unraveling the process a bit more, I learned that a strong Second-in-Command had previously been part of the review process. This explained why prior submissions had been accepted without question. Unfortunately, some senior leaders did not fully appreciate the value of the verification process when a reorganization took place, moving the 2iC to a new role. This was the first data submission that she had not been part of.

Even having verification systems in place does not eliminate the need for all verification reviews. Since Seconds-in-Command are constantly taking in information that enables them to spot errors and potential issues, a 2iC review can add a level of quality approaching Six Sigma. As a result of the events described above, the Second-in-Command was asked to re-engage in the verification process for high-stakes deliverables.

In this particular case, a small coding error had excluded some customers. The error could easily have been caught with the question "Approximately how many customers should we expect to be on the list, based on other known numbers?" The amount was off by half, an easy-to-spot issue for an experienced 2iC.

Even a small error in the code can result in information that is incomplete or even wrong. In this case, it was a nuance that the developer could not have known about. The caveat was not part of her data requirements request. It was an honest oversight.

Accuracy Requires Being in the Right Headspace

It's even more frustrating when mistakes are sloppy due to work being rushed and corners cut. Sloppy work is when people are moving through a task so quickly that they just don't seem to care about quality anymore and are not really watching what they're doing. As a Second-in-Command, you never know when somebody is having a bad day and has made some sloppy mistakes. But we all know that everyone has bad days, so 2iCs need to be attentive to the headspace that employees are in as it will impact their work. Recognizing when employees are not performing at their best is part of the 2iC's role. This information can be used to know when to do a preliminary or more thorough review of the deliverables, ensuring quality despite the bad day.

It's not just about finding the mistake and certainly not about being punitive about it. It's about utilizing the verification findings as a retrospective teaching moment for the whole team to understand where these mistakes are coming from so that they can improve moving forward. This time, it was the developer who made an error in the code. Next time it could be the person who was writing the report that misinterpreted what the data point meant or inverted the numbers.

Take Action—Progress Over Perfection

Questions for Reflection and Discussion

1. What is the most common reason you find inaccurate information? How do you mitigate it?
2. What do you do when you receive wrong information? What do you do to ensure that the same mistake is not made again?
3. What is a time when you relied on information you received and later found out it had been incorrect? What did that mean for the project? (e.g., rework, reputation loss, canceled project, etc.)
4. What is your process to verify information before making decisions or submitting the information to your First-in-Command?
5. What process does your First-in-Command use to verify information? Can you adopt their process such that the deliverable arrives pre-verified?

Stage 11

Crosschecking

As Seconds-in-Command, we are constantly building. We take parts and assemble them into something new that fulfills a need or solves a problem. However, the process of building doesn't always come easily.

Take, for example, assembling a simple piece of furniture. Many of us have purchased a desk or chair that requires assembly. Like any shopper, we find a product we like that will fit into the available space and is within our desired price range.

When the box arrives at our home, we open it up to find the furniture in many pieces, along with what looks like 1,000 bolts, washers, and nuts. After finding the directions buried in the box, we begin with the first step. And like most directions—whether it be for assembly, work, or life—they are enough to get the job done but lack helpful details that would have made the process a lot easier.

It is about this time that most people will think, "Thank goodness for the picture on the box; at least we know what we are trying to build and how it should look." Just imagine what we all would end up with if we didn't have the picture or goal in mind!

DOI: 10.4324/9781003382003-16

As a form of crosschecking, nearing the assembly completion, we begin to look around to make sure we have used all of the parts, including the hardware. Most furniture assembly packages come with an extra bolt, nut, or washer or two. The manufacturer does this to reduce the number of returns and unhappy customers who might not be able to complete the assembly due to losing a piece of hardware or receiving one fewer than needed. However, the directions rarely note how many and what type of extra hardware pieces are included. As a result, the assembler is left wondering, "Did I put a washer on that last bolt?" "Did I use the right size bolt six steps ago?"

Thus, we go back and check our work. "Does it look like the picture?" "Are there any holes that should have bolts but don't?" "Does the furniture look sturdy or stable?" We are crosschecking not only for the hardware but also for other things, such as overall quality and any damage that might have occurred during shipping.

In Stage 11 of the 2iC Excellence Framework (Figure 23), I focus on crosschecking every which way.

Crosschecking: What It Means in Practice

Although working in compliance has a lot of disadvantages, there are also many advantages. For example, when an annual financial audit is taking place, the auditors obviously review the content that they are given. However, more sophisticated and thorough audit firms will also review the absence of information. This seems really hard and weird. How can you review something that isn't there? The firm is crosschecking that information hasn't been left out of the audit file. This section includes three lesser-used methods for crosschecking to add to your 2iC tool kit: the absence of information, a

Figure 23 2iC Excellence Framework—Crosscheck—Stage 11.

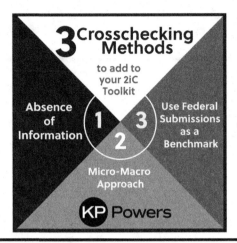

Figure 24 Three Crosschecking Methods to Add To Your 2iC Toolkit.

micro-macro approach, and using federal submissions as a benchmark (Figure 24).

The Absence of Information

When I first encountered the concept of "absence of information" through an audit firm, I was a bit taken aback. I thought that they didn't trust me. How was I supposed to show information that wasn't there? How was I supposed to produce information that didn't exist? For this particular audit, I needed to pull all records so that the review team could determine if any customers had been left out. The audit firm was testing the entire population in addition to the file extract to ensure that the customers in the file extract were included or excluded accurately.

In this project, I had been completely focused on the details and all of the columns and pieces of information. My focus on the data pull was so strong that I failed to take a moment to ask myself, "Is this the right result? Is this the number of students that we were expecting in the population for the audit? Are these the right pieces of information to satisfy the data request? Does the information make sense? Are the values in each of the cells even plausible? For example, does the ZIP Code column contain a five-digit number?"

Crosschecking means really thinking about the project from multiple angles. Of course, vertically and horizontally are two directions, but there are also other directions, such as crisscross, diagonal, and all four corners. The idea is to really pressure-test the task.

A Micro-Macro Approach

Ask, "If I were a fresh reader looking at this one piece of information, would I find it confusing, problematic, or easy to understand?" This micro-macro approach of digging into the details while still being able to look at the big picture results in higher quality deliverables. It allows the Second-in-Command to review the final product from multiple perspectives, simulating the review that the next set of readers will do.

It may be useful to think about the first three questions a reader would ask and then go back and make sure that those questions have been answered. If it's a data file, can you pivot out the data, looking for outliers on each one of the variables and plausible values? For example, are the numbers within an expected range? Do the values make sense for the variable?

Using Federal Submissions as a Benchmark

Having done a lot of federal compliance work throughout my career, I have learned that federal submissions often receive a lot more attention than internal data and information requests. Since these reports have undergone such a rigorous review, I utilize them as a benchmark or a comparison point. For example, if the number of employees was reported to the federal government for a certain period of time, I can use that number as a barometer when comparing for a subset.

If an organization reported having 1,000 employees and the internal request is looking for one particular department, if I know that particular department is one of the largest, I'm going to expect that it will be a high number. Similarly, if it's a small department, I'm going to expect it to be a relatively small number.

Existing and already vetted external reports can serve as a resource and a tool for crosschecking.

The Value of Crosschecking

We all want to be known for doing good work and take pride in providing our organization with high-quality deliverables. While it takes a bit of extra time to crosscheck, it's worth it to ensure accuracy. More importantly, it's worth it to protect your reputation as an employee. As a Second-in-Command, you not only want to show that you do good work by crosschecking to prepare information for the First-in-Command but also teach others how to improve the quality of the information they are providing to you. It's important not to leave crosschecking entirely to someone else because it can affect your reputation and the quality of the work that you're delivering.

"Collaborative crosschecking is a strategy where at least two individuals or groups with different perspectives examine the others' assumptions and/or actions to assess validity or accuracy. With this strategy, erroneous assessments or actions can be detected quickly enough to mitigate or eliminate negative consequences" (Patterson, Woods, Cook, & Render, 2007, p. 1).

Unlike verifying, crosschecking is part of your role as a Second-in-Command. This responsibility cannot be delegated, outsourced, or replaced with technology. You need to become a past master at crosschecking so that you can catch things well before they go down the line and cause problems.

Many Seconds-in-Command are involved with budgets. They might manage a department budget, develop financial models, or review organization financials. As part of the crosschecking process, 2iCs are looking at each line in the context of the other lines as well as information that they know from other sources. For example, does it make sense that office supplies are 40% of the budget? Is the revenue estimate a reasonable number such that it includes new products or services? 2iCs are looking to see if the numbers are within the expected ranges. A good way to know is to ask, "What number is available to compare this to?" Comparisons can include prior year numbers (if available), publicly available data points, and percentages of the total on the spreadsheet.

Benefits of Crosschecking

Part of the crosscheck is looking at things in different ways than others who might also be reviewing the materials to catch errors that you would not have identified had you just gone through the spreadsheet linearly. As Second-in-Command, it's important not only that you take the time to crosscheck but also that you think of creative ways to cross-check information points so that you will unearth errors that you would have missed if you had just started from the beginning.

Think about how to turn it on its side, read it upside-down, and look at it backward—any technique that you can use to help you find things that you might overlook because you've been staring at the document for too long or because someone told you that it had already been reviewed. You have to have your own ways to ferret out some of those errors.

Figure Out What Your 1iC Will Want to Know

Your First-in-Command is skilled at asking questions and is not shy about it. Take note of what questions they are asking because that's their way of verifying. As part of your cross-checking process, ask yourself questions similar to those your First-in-Command would ask. Role-play through the answers to see if there are ways to improve the quality of the deliverable even further.

Doing this type of role-playing will help you beat the First-in-Command to the questions they were going to ask and make sure that you already have the answers and have already addressed any related issues. The First-in-Command will realize that their questions are no longer probing deep enough because you've already addressed them. Having anticipated their questions will push them to go further. In the end, both of you will have leveled up.

Take Action—Progress Over Perfection

Questions for Reflection and Discussion

1. How has crosschecking built relationships and trust in your projects as a 2iC?
2. What are the most significant challenges you have had when crosschecking?
3. How have others crosschecked your work? Can you utilize some of those strategies in crosschecking others work in your 2iC role?
4. Recall a time when some information was not cross-checked with another key stakeholder or department. What were the results? What should have been done differently?

Stage 12

Protecting Your #1

In golf, caddies are there to look out for and protect the golfer (aka the #1). Of course, caddies know how to golf, so they could easily aim to be a #1 themselves.

Some golf caddies have elected to fully embrace their 2iC role. Their focus is on selecting the best club for the golfer to use in a particular set of circumstances so that the golfer can focus exclusively on making the shot. If the golfer has to think about the different club options and the slope and the weather and the wind, they will not be able to concentrate as much on the shot.

> A great caddie is more than a bag carrier; he is a motivator, encourager, admonisher, counselor, and advisor. He is there with you every day to coach while you are practicing and when you are playing. Good caddies understand your strengths and weaknesses and your stress and anxiety cycles, such as how you are affected by pressure, adrenaline, winning and losing, and they guide you through those emotional moments.
>
> (Gaborit, 2022)

DOI: 10.4324/9781003382003-17

As a Second-in-Command, you are trying to remove all possible distractions so that the First-in-Command can focus on the things you can't do for them. The 12th and final Stage in the 2iC Excellence Framework is Protecting Your #1 (Figure 25).

Protecting Your #1: What It Means in Action

Time is really limited, especially for Firsts-in-Command. Often they are the only people who can do a particular task, especially in smaller organizations. For example, Firsts-in-Command need to meet with investors to close deals, meet with the board, and deliver a speech that shares goals for the year.

The more the #1 can progress with their work rather than getting distracted or pulled off course on another topic or in the weeds, the better for everybody. Therefore, one of the Second-in-Command's critical responsibilities is to prevent people and things from detracting from the #1's focus. The Dean of the United States University College of Education, Rebecca Wardlow, explains it this way,

> I always want to lessen the burden for my First-in-Command; I want to simplify their life. I also want to meet their goals and care for the people that I work with and for and work for me.

This stage of protecting the #1 centers on getting information to the #1 before the #1 has even asked for it, as well as identifying opportunities to streamline the #1's schedule so that they can fully concentrate on their goals. Additionally, the 2iC needs to serve as a truth-teller to the #1 so that the #1 can properly address problems and issues before they get too large.

Figure 25 2iC Excellence Framework—Protect Your #1—Stage 12.

The Value of Protecting Your #1

The First-in-Command has a ton of skill sets and expertise. Like the #1, the Second-in-Command has a unique role. The Second-in-Command is doing work that is highly valued by the #1, not only from a time, effort, energy, and money standpoint, but also because in many cases, the #1 recognizes that it is not in their wheelhouse and would take them a much longer to do on their own.

Firsts-in-Command quickly figure out they can accomplish much more with the help of a Second-in-Command. It's not just about having a second person; it's about having somebody who is a Second-in-Command with all of the associated skill sets shown in the infinity loop.

Part of the role of a 2iC is protecting the First-in-Command by catching upcoming issues or errors before they become real issues or errors. One of the reasons many 2iCs are so successful with their Firsts-in-Command is that they often are a go-to resource for just about everything.

Jacquie Furtado, Director of Strategy & Outcomes at San Diego State University's Academy for Professional Excellence, shared,

> In addition to building trust, when I felt I was most productive and where I contributed the most is when I had a strong relationship with my first in command. During those times, I felt that I could bring my authentic self to work every day. I was trusted to work autonomously. But I still had a feedback loop and the ability to lead with inquiry to ask questions: what's working, what's not, and how can I help you?

Firsts-in-Command are first for a reason. They are CEOs, founders, and visionaries. However, just because they are good at forward-thinking doesn't mean they are good at everything—nor that they want to be. Often Firsts-in-Command are so consumed by their role that they need and want a Second-in-Command to take on more of the details.

Benefits of Protecting Your #1

Just like anyone, Firsts-in-Command can have bad days. Some can have many bad days in a row, making them challenging to work with occasionally. Others in the organization know that you work closely with First-in-Command and may seek out your input or advice on the best ways to work with the #1.

In the process, they may say negative comments to you about the First-in-Command. As part of protecting your #1, it is important that you not entertain or allow those comments. It doesn't matter if you agree with them or not; keep the conversation focused on how best to work with the First-in-Command. Protecting the reputation of the First-in-Command also goes along with this role.

Seconds-in-Command in Sports: Football

Our second example from the world of sports is linemen, who fulfill a 2iC role by protecting the quarterback (First-in-Command). Similar to the golf caddy in the introduction to this section, linemen know how to do the role of their First-in-Command. They want the quarterback to be able to focus on throwing the ball and not worry about any of the other opposing players that are coming close. Of course, the quarterback knows what the linemen are doing for him, but he isn't paying attention to the details.

Sonali Kothari, Founder of Zolidar & Executive Coach, Kothari Leadership, describes the relationship this way:

> As a Second-in-Command, I am figuring out my role within the context of the First-in-Command. Rather than trying to change that person or trying to get them to give me what I need, I concentrate on trying to figure out what the First-in-Command is trying to achieve. And then how do I support their goals within my role while not giving up my desires or values?

2iCs in Travel

A 2iC that I know was in the group travel industry. The First-in-Command had retired, and so the Second-in-Command moved up into their position. The first year, she tried to do the First-in-Command role on her own. While she did a great job overall, there were some pinch points (e.g., missed dead-lines, late payments from participants). Observing these challenges, a colleague offered their assistance as Second-in-Command, working on the details. This 2iC had no interest in being the First-in-Command.

The 2iC quickly ascertained that finances were not the First-in-Command's strong suit. Of course, she wanted to be sure the group trip did not lose money. The 2iC, who was skilled in finance, saw an opportunity to protect the #1 by having a balanced budget and jumped in on the budget to take the lead. The 2iC followed up on late payments from participants, sent payment reminders to travelers, and provided the First-in-Command with a budget and financial update without even being asked.

Now the First-in-Command only runs the trip with her 2iC, not only because the two of them have their processes worked out of who does what but mostly because she truly enjoys being supported by the 2iC, who takes care of protecting her time, looking out for issues, and crosschecking.

Take Action—Progress Over Perfection

Questions for Reflection and Discussion

1. What are some ways, as a 2iC, try to make it easier for your First-in-Command to do their work? What type of response do you get when utilizing those strategies? What is the impact on the goals?
2. How do you prevent others from distracting or detouring the First-in-Command away from their job?
3. What approaches do you use to tell your #1 bad news?

BLAZING NEW TRAILS

The work of leaders is never complete. There is always something to improve. Further, there are new trails to blaze. Many leaders enjoy the consistency of inconsistency—no two projects are the same, and there are always new things to try or address.

In this last section of the book, there are two chapters to address 2iCs who are blazing new trails through:

- Emergency Planning
- Forming Second-in-Command Chains

DOI: 10.4324/9781003382003-18

Emergency Planning

Emergency rooms do urgent work all the time—that is literally their purpose. Think about the last time that you were in the emergency room. It was probably for a long time. The medical staff performs the same medical procedures that one would expect at a doctor's office (e.g., taking blood pressure and temperature, asking questions, getting a blood sample) but at a more rapid pace.

In interviews for this book, many Seconds-in-Command talked about how they assisted their organization and Firsts-in-Command during an emergency, quick turnaround projects, and rapid-fire projects. In this last part of the 2iC Excellence Framework, the focus is on emergency planning (Figure 26). There are always emergencies and quick-fire drills at any organization. Very few people like to plan to avoid emergencies. Perhaps that's why it feels like there are so many of them.

Emergency Planning: What It Means in Action

It's important for a Second-in-Command to be able to work through emergencies as fast as possible. Responding to emergencies is simply accelerated planning. For example, if you knew that the computer servers would go down on a certain

DOI: 10.4324/9781003382003-19

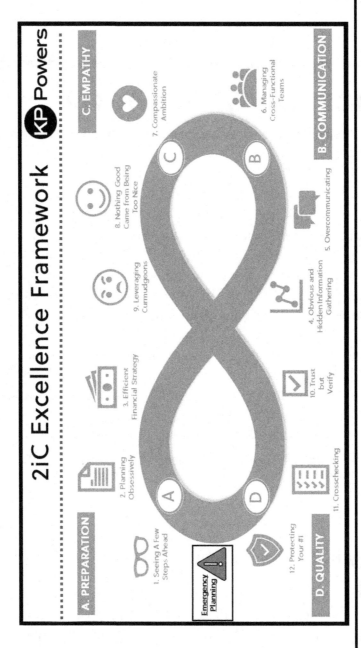

Figure 26   2iC Excellence Framework—Emergency Planning.

date, you would do some advance planning to let customers and staff members know. When the computer servers go down without notice due to a technology failure or power outage, the steps to restore the systems are the same; they just need to be completed very quickly. As a 2iC, the better you can get at emergency planning, the better prepared you will be for emergencies when they come up. And they always come up.

Seconds-in-Command can improve their emergency planning skills by moving through the infinity diagram repeatedly, getting faster and more precise each time. For every iteration through the infinity loop, the 2iC is not relearning each Stage but rather returning to each Stage with the knowledge gained from all of the previous trips around the loop.

Focusing on making decisions quickly at a time that's already stressful can be very difficult. The more times that you go through the infinity process, the better able you will be to plan quickly to manage emergencies.

On a day when there isn't an emergency, decisions can be difficult. Add in an emergency and the difficulty of decisions is amplified. "People don't understand the complexities of decision-making," explains Stacey Gonzales, Ed.D., education leader

> Oftentimes, there's a lot of confidential information that you maybe can't even share. As a Second-in-Command, you are there to really serve as a thought partner, allowing space to think through different options and their implications.

The Value of Emergency Planning

Costly Rework and Late Work

Rework and late work are costly. Redoing the same work that has already been done is both frustrating and expensive.

Rarely does rework result in a better-quality product or service because redoing and fixing something is a different skill set than doing it right the first time.

For example, 2iCs often analyze a lot of data and information to synthesize it for their First-in-Command. As part of the review, you may find content that conflicts within the document or with established truths. Part of your role as a Second-in-Command is to either obtain additional clarification or send the document back to be corrected.

Either way, additional time is needed to rework the deliverable before it can be shared with the First-in-Command. When reworking, employees feel rushed because they know that the deliverable was needed yesterday. Additionally, fixing work that has already been done introduces fatigue because the employee is not utilizing their normal processes. As a result, the opportunity for more errors increases.

Late work is similar but carries additional stress and typically a penalty. The penalty could be financial. For example, submitting a compliance report late to the federal or state government could include a late fee. Internally, completing a deliverable late could result in more intangible penalties such as diminished reputation or reduced trust for future projects. It might even hurt one's chances for a promotion.

Fixing the Problem So It Doesn't Get Bigger

Once a problem is known, it is important to address it immediately. Doing so reduces the likelihood of the problem getting worse. Additionally, the longer a problem goes unattended, the more costly it can be to fix it and the greater the likelihood of irreversible damage.

For example, when technology systems go down, it is important to get them up and running as soon as possible. That's why most organizations develop protocols to ensure a timely response through the use of on-call employees and/or phone trees. Timely response by individuals who can fix the problem can make the difference between a minor issue and a catastrophe.

Tiffany Paine-Cirrincione, Director of Development and Communications at St. Joseph's Neighborhood Center, shared,

> I've learned as a leader not to be married to the leader or the decision maker. Rather, it is better to be married to the mission and to the people you serve. Because that allows me to be flexible when it comes to whose idea something is or whose idea we execute or how we do something. My goal is to focus on the endpoint and make sure that it gets done.

In the finance industry, time is literally money. When critical finance systems that are responsible for stock trading go down, every minute counts. Since the price of stocks varies throughout the day, a few hours difference in submitting a trade can have a significant financial impact, not to mention violate federal laws regarding timely trading.

Benefits of Emergency Planning

Whatever name your organization might have for these accelerated projects, the processes and the skill sets are those identified in the infinity loop and the 12 stages in this book— at an expedited pace. It is during emergencies that a Second-in-Command can leverage all of their 2iC skill sets simultaneously.

2iCs move through the infinity diagram at a rapid pace. Because they have been through the process multiple times, it gets easier and easier to move through it more and more quickly. Seconds-in-Command often find themselves among the first to be called for emergency situations because of their unique ability to make progress during the crisis while maintaining their calm and professionalism.

The 2iC's skill sets are at their most valuable, and the First-in-Command really needs them during these stressful times. It is in times of crisis that many employees look to leadership to provide pathways to stability. In these difficult moments, trust and relationships are strengthened when the Second-in-Command manages each of the 12 stages in the infinity loop, especially the three components in the empathy Stage.

Take Action—Progress Over Perfection

Questions for Reflection and Discussion

1. What are the steps you would take to improve emergency planning for your company?
2. Knowing that emergencies will happen—they are unavoidable—how have you prepared for emergencies over your career?
3. What is an experience from your past that has helped guide you in a moment of crisis?
4. What do you think the most important piece of emergency preparedness is?
5. What was the most unexpected emergency that you had to deal with and how did you handle it? How has it made you a better 2iC?

Forming Second-in-Command Chains

What Is a 2iC Chain?

In a 2iC chain, two or more Seconds-in-Command are linked with a 1iC. A chain of 2iCs is even more powerful than a single 2iC, creating the potential for a 10× impact (see Figure 2: Value of a 2iC Chain in the chapter "Why This Book?").

The Value of Forming Second-in-Command Chains

Throughout my career as a 2iC, I've noticed that unintentional 2iC chains can and do develop. Although many leaders are still used to an outdated management style with only one Second-in-Command, such as a chief operating officer or chief of staff, larger and more complex organizations have discovered the value of having multiple 2iCs. For example, Fortune 500 companies have a chief operating officer, *and* most divisions within these companies each have a chief of staff (e.g., each executive vice president has their own chief of

DOI: 10.4324/9781003382003-20

staff). Since organizations are already employing multiple 2iCs, it makes sense to put some purposeful intention and effort into creating a strategy for determining how many Seconds-in-Command are needed and where they should sit.

Benefits of Forming Second-in-Command Chains

Moving Through the Infinity Loop Multiple Times

As a Second-in-Command, you've likely been through the infinity loop multiple times. And each time, you learn something new. No step or Stage ever feels quite the same. Each lap is completely different because you're approaching it with a new set of experiences under your belt.

Eventually, you will master the infinity loop. But the challenges will continue to become more refined and increase in complexity. As that complexity increases, the scope of work will grow too, especially once you are able to move rapidly through the infinity loop. Seconds-in-Command reach a point where they could benefit from a Second-in Command of their own and are ready to teach and mentor others to serve in the role. Being a Second-in-Command with a Second in Command can require some mental gymnastics. It feels a little luxurious at first.

You might even think, "Who am I to have a Second-in-Command of my own?" Rather than thinking about your 2iC being exclusively for you, think about their support as the multiplier that allows you to perform your job at a higher level, which then has a domino effect for your First-in-Command. This 2iC chain can make it possible to complete work, tackle projects, and achieve goals that would otherwise be too ambitious.

2iC Chain—Encore

While the 2iC Chain was introduced in an earlier chapter, the following few paragraphs bear repeating for two reasons: (1) so you won't have to look back in the book to find a few key paragraphs and (2) it is a new concept for many, so repetition helps reinforce.

In a 2iC Chain, two or more Seconds-in-Command are linked together with a First-in-Command. A chain of 2iCs has an even more powerful effect than a single 2iC, creating the potential for a 10X impact (Figure 27).

I have had the privilege of being part of multiple 2iC chains. The results have been nothing short of phenomenal— and among the best experiences of my professional life. The following are two examples:

- **Middle Circle as 2iC**: I held a senior leadership position as the 2iC to the president while a member of my team served as a 2iC to me, creating a multiplying effect. The three of us combined accomplished phenomenal results.

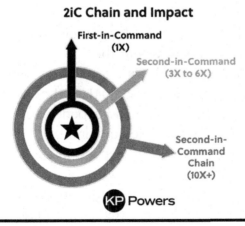

2iC Chain and Impact

First-in-Command (1X)

Second-in-Command (3X to 6X)

Second-in-Command Chain (10X+)

KP Powers

Figure 27   Second-in-Command (2iC) Chain and Impact With Star.

- **Outer Circle as 2iC**: I served as a 2iC to the 2iC to the president. Being the last link in a 2iC chain gave me a new perspective on the 2iC chain and its importance. Acting as a 2iC to another 2iC creates incredible momentum for accomplishing big goals with passion.

How to Identify Potential Seconds-in-Command

There are early indicators that can help you identify potential 2iCs. The ideal candidates are highly motivated to take on a Second-in-Command role and have demonstrated skill with one or more of the 12 stages in the 2iC Excellence Framework on previous projects.

I use a quadrant model (Figure 28) with two axes—motivation and skill set—to help categorize existing and potential 2iCs.

- 2iC In-Practice: Individuals in this quadrant are ideally suited to officially move into a 2iC role, assuming they aren't already in one. Their combination of high motivation and great skill sets makes these employees obvious choices and very easy to identify. While most of them will perform well in the 2iC role, they can benefit from more formal training and professional development specifically for 2iCs to multiply their and their First-in-Command's impact even further.
- Willing, Not Able: Individuals in this quadrant have high motivation to become a 2iC but lack the skill sets. However, with more formal training and experience, they could move into the 2iC in the Practice quadrant. Employees in this quadrant are interested in Second-in-Command responsibilities but won't yet be effective at fulfilling them. Some curmudgeons may belong in this quadrant.
- Able, Not Willing: Employees in this quadrant have a high 2iC skill set because they are already practicing many of the 2iC stages. For example, they may be able to

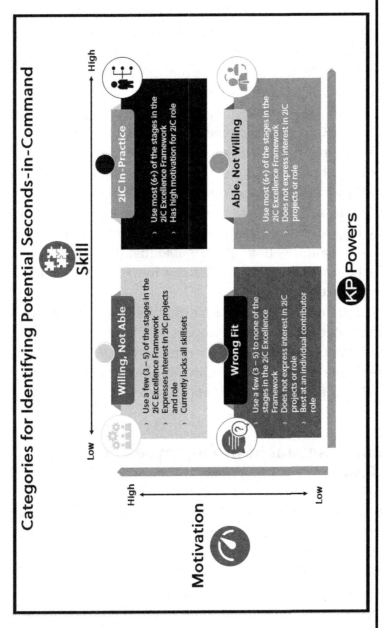

Figure 28 Categories for Identifying Potential Seconds-in-Command.

see ahead and have compassionate ambition. However, they have zero or low interest in taking on a Second-in-Command role. These are folks who tend to be steady, stable forces in an organization. They simply don't want to be a 2iC. Their reluctance may be due to one of two reasons: (1) they do not see the value or (2) the value does not align with their goals.

It may be possible to move individuals in this quadrant to the 2iC in Practice quadrant by providing motivators for serving in the role, such as the ability to impact the organization, an expanded scope of work, or a pathway to a First-in-Command role. Being a 2iC may not align with the employee's current goals. Perhaps they have family responsibilities that don't allow them to embrace that role fully at this time. It's possible that they might have higher motivation at a later point in their career at the organization.

• Wrong Fit: The 2iC role isn't right for everyone, so it's inevitable that some employees will land in the Wrong Fit quadrant. There's nothing wrong with that. This exercise is simply intended to identify employees who already are a 2iC in practice or could move into that category.

Annual Assessment of Employees for the 2iC Role

It is useful to do the quadrant assessment annually because employee placement can change over time as family and life circumstances evolve or new leadership comes in. Organizations can easily incorporate it into employee talent reviews or annual employee evaluations.

It is important to note that each employee is not simply in a quadrant; they are in a particular part of that quadrant. For example, in Figure 29, some employees are close to a

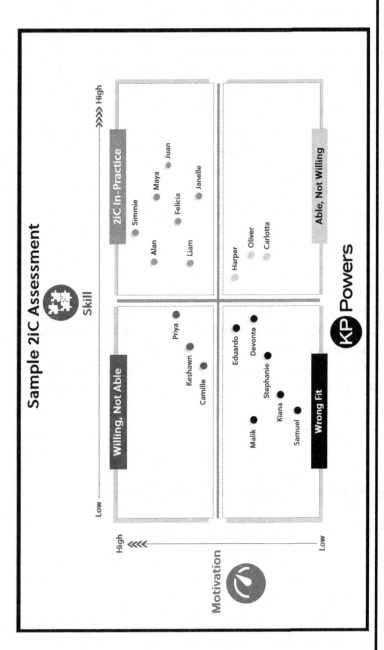

Figure 29   Sample 2iC Assessment.

dividing line, while others are squarely in the middle of the quadrant. By taking the time to place employees at the most appropriate spot within their particular quadrant and relative to other employees, an organization can get a clear picture of current and potential Second-in-Command availability.

Whether you are introducing and/or expanding 2iCs and 2iC chains at your organization, remember that it is a marathon, not a sprint. Yes, you can accelerate the implementation of 2iCs, 2iC chains, and the 2iC Excellence Framework. However, just as with any new initiative, it takes practice to reach full results.

It takes time to practice. Many leaders are impatient (myself included). We all want results yesterday. That's why it's important to begin the implementation process today—don't wait until tomorrow.

You can begin on your own with the quadrant exercise (Figures 28 and 29). And when you are ready to go further, let's connect. You can find out ways to connect with me in the Let's Connect section at the back of this book.

Until then, I wish you phenomenal success on your 2iC and 2iC chain journey and look forward to hearing about your successes, challenges, and ideas as a result of using the 2iC Excellence Framework.

Take Action—Progress Over Perfection

Questions for Reflection and Discussion

1. How many 2iCs do you have? Where do they sit?
2. Do you know what other executives at your company have multiple Seconds-in-Command?
3. In what ways do you see your organization benefiting from using multiple Seconds-in-Command?

4. As the organization grows, what are some factors to consider when deciding if you need another Second-in-Command? (e.g., size of the company, revenue, customer satisfaction, desire to innovate).
5. As a leadership team, go through the process of identifying potential Seconds-in-Command (see Figures 28 and 29).
   a. What insights came up?
   b. What opportunities to leverage your talent became evident?
   c. What three actions will you take today to advance the use of Seconds-in-Command at your organization?

References

Gaborit, C. (2022). *3 Leadership Lessons from the World's Greatest Caddie*. LinkedIn. https://www.linkedin.com/pulse/3-leadership-lessons-from-worlds-greatest-caddie-chris-gaborit/

Grammarly. (2022). *The State of Business Communication*. https://www.grammarly.com/business/Grammarly_The_State_Of_Business_Communication.pdf

Hait, A. (2021). *The Majority of U.S. Businesses Have Fewer Than Five Employees*. U.S. Census Bureau. https://www.census.gov/library/stories/2021/01/what-is-a-small-business.html

Jordan, S. (2020). *5 Strategy Development Tips for Small Businesses in 2020*. Clutch. https://clutch.co/consulting/resources/strategy-development-tips-small-businesses?

Patterson, E.S., Woods, D.D., Cook, R.I. et al. Collaborative cross-checking to enhance resilience. *Cogn Tech Work* 9, 155–162 (2007). https://doi.org/10.1007/s10111-006-0054-8

Platinum Group (2020). Strategic planning: The key to profitability in business. https://www.platinum-grp.com/blog/strategic-planning-why-it-is-critical-for-business-success

Vopson, M. M. (2021). *The world's data explained: How much we're producing and where it's all stored*. https://theconversation.com/the-worlds-data-explained-how-much-were-producing-and-where-its-all-stored-159964

Wiles, J. (2021). *Great Resignation or Not, Money Won't Fix All Your Talent Problems*. Gartner. https://www.gartner.com/en/articles/great-resignation-or-not-money-won-t-fix-all-your-talent-problems

Young Entrepreneur Council. (2022). *8 Predictions for How the Workforce Will Change in 2023*. https://www.inc.com/young-entrepreneur-council/8-predictions-for-how-workforce-will-change-in-2023.html

Let's Connect

Relationships are the bedrock for accomplishment. They are critical to doing the Second-in-Command role well. Part of having relationships includes building new ones, and I don't mean through likes and follows on social media; I mean real connections through dialogue and/or working on a project to achieve phenomenal results.

If you've made it to the end of this book, you are among the 1% of readers of all books who check out the back matter. I love building relationships with other overachievers (we make each other better). Therefore, I'm inviting you to connect with me. Here's how:

- **Email me**: Yep! You can email me directly at KP@ KPPowers.com I read all of my emails. I would love to hear what you've learned and applied from this book as well as challenges and ideas you've had as a result of reading and applying information from the book. What topics resonated with you? What leadership levers are you looking for even more information on? How has the content impacted your role? Others at your work?
- **Let's work together**: I offer accelerator programs for leaders and organizations that want to achieve phenomenal results. I love working with ambitious leaders that set high goals. Working together on a project is the

fastest way to build relationships, and there is the added benefit of accomplishing goals and achieving phenomenal results.

- **Join my newsletter**: My newsletter is called Knowledge is Powers. Every two to three weeks I send out content on what I'm thinking about, trends I'm noticing, stories that inspire me, and updates on new books, trainings, and workshops. Occasionally I take a few weeks off from the newsletter for big projects—like writing a book. You can join me on my website, www.KPPowers.com/ newsletter.

- **Engage with me on social**: As social media continues to evolve, I'm always checking out new platforms. Therefore, the social media outlets that I'm currently using are updated and on my website. Join one or more of your favorites. I'd love for you not just to follow me on social media but so we can build a relationship. I read and respond to comments on my social media.

I look forward to connecting with you.

KP

KP@KPPowers.com
www.KPPowers.com

Index

Pages in *italics* refer to figures.

Printed in the United States
by Baker & Taylor Publisher Services